DOONESBURY NATION

Recent Doonesbury Books by G.B. Trudeau

Read My Lips, Make My Day, Eat Quiche and Die!
Give Those Nymphs Some Hooters!
You're Smokin' Now, Mr. Butts!
I'd Go With the Helmet, Ray
Welcome to Club Scud!
What Is It, Tink, Is Pan in Trouble?
Quality Time on Highway 1
Washed Out Bridges and Other Disasters
In Search of Cigarette Holder Man

In Large Format

The Doonesbury Chronicles
Doonesbury's Greatest Hits
The People's Doonesbury
Doonesbury Dossier: The Reagan Years
Doonesbury Deluxe: Selected Glances Askance
Recycled Doonesbury: Second Thoughts on a Gilded Age
Action Figure!
The Portable Doonesbury

A DOONESBURY BOOK

by G. B. TRUDEAU

DOONESBURY NATION

ANDREWS and McMEEL — A UNIVERSAL PRESS SYNDICATE COMPANY — KANSAS CITY

DOONESBURY is distributed internationally by Universal Press Syndicate.

ISBN: 0-8362-1784-5

Library of Congress Catalog Card Number: 94-72812

"It's nothing but these ex-hippies making money that they were too high to make the first time."

— Punk-rocker Henry Rollins

LITTLE CHURCH OF WALDEN
OKAY, FLOCK. I THOUGHT I'D RUN THROUGH THIS WEEK'S ACTIVITIES...

THIS MONDAY, OF COURSE, WE HAVE A LECTURE ON NUTRITION FROM KATE MOSS' PERSONAL CHEF...

TUESDAY AND THURSDAY WILL BE OUR REGULAR 12-STEP NIGHTS...
SCOT, WOULD THAT BE DRUGS OR SEX ADDICTION?

DRUGS. SEX ADDICTION WE'VE CUT DOWN TO NINE STEPS. THAT'S ON FRIDAY AT 6:30 P.M.— RIGHT AFTER ORGANIC CO-GARDENING...

ALSO, A SPECIAL TREAT— SATURDAY NIGHT WILL BE AEROBIC MALE-BONDING NIGHT! SO BRING YOUR SNEAKS! ANY QUESTIONS?

YES, IS THERE A CHURCH SERVICE?
CANCELLED. THERE WAS A CONFLICT WITH THE SELF-ESTEEM WORKSHOP.
©B Trudeau

CONTROL, THIS IS SENTRY. SECTOR B HAS BEEN STERILIZED. OVER.
COPY THAT, SENTRY. GUARDIAN?

THIS IS GUARDIAN. SECTOR C ALL CLEAR.
PAYDAY, THIS IS CONTROL. MESS AREA IS SECURE. ENJOY YOUR BREAKFAST, COLONEL.

FLOP!
FLOP!

HEY... SOMETHING'S WRONG! THIS MUFFIN'S BEEN TAMPERED WITH!
YOUR WIFE BUTTERED IT, SIR.

COLONEL NORTH, YOUR 0930 APPOINTMENT IS HERE—RICK REDFERN FROM THE POST...

GOOD. HERE'S THE DRILL. BURST IN ON US AFTER FIVE MINUTES AND ANNOUNCE THAT MY WIFE WILL "WRING MY NECK" IF I'M LATE TO MY NEXT EVENT.
GOT IT, SIR.

THAT SHOULD CONTAIN THE INTERVIEW. WHERE IS HE NOW?
HE'S CLEARING SECURITY, SIR.

OKAY, NOW TURN AROUND!
FORGET IT.

COLONEL NORTH, EARLY IN YOUR CAMPAIGN, YOU LIKED TO SAY THAT THE ONLY THING YOU WERE RUNNING FOR WAS "HUSBAND AND FATHER..."

AFFIRMATIVE. FAMILY TIME IS PRECIOUS. THE GOOD LORD LOANED ME FOUR CHILDREN—AND MY BEST FRIEND, BETSY.

YOU MEAN YOUR WIFE?
YES. SHE, TOO, IS ONLY A LOANER.

AND YOUR NEW COUNTRY ESTATE?
NO, THAT I OWN OUTRIGHT.

SIR, DON'T YOU FIND IT A BIT STRANGE TO BE RUNNING FOR THE SAME CONGRESS YOU WERE CONVICTED OF LYING TO?
NOT AT ALL.

THE FACT IS I'VE NEVER BEEN CON-VICTED OF ANY CRIME AT ALL...
UH-OH...

THE SYSTEM FOUND ME NOT GUILTY!
COLONEL? HEADS UP— YOU'RE LYING.
©B Trudeau

I AM?
YES, SIR, YOU SAID TO LET YOU KNOW.

SEE, WHAT WE'VE GOT ARE THESE PERMANENT POTENTATES OF PORK WHO NEVER LEAVE THIS SAD SWAMP THAT MEN CALL WASHINGTON, D.C.!

WELL, THAT RAISES AN INTERESTING QUESTION, COLONEL. IF YOU HAVE SUCH CONTEMPT FOR CONGRESS, WHY DO YOU WANT TO JOIN IT?

IT'S NOT A QUESTION OF WHAT I WANT. BELIEVE ME, I'D RATHER BE LEADING A BATTALION INTO HARM'S WAY AT THE OUTER EDGE OF THE EMPIRE—BUT THE LORD HAS OTHER PLANS FOR ME!
©B Trudeau

SO IT WAS GOD WHO FIRST SUGGESTED...
IT WAS A DIRECT ORDER! LET ME EXPLAIN...
UH-OH...

BUT AREN'T YOU, IN EFFECT, CALLING REAGAN A LIAR, SIR?
UH-OH, BETTER CUT THIS OFF...
OH, COLONEL?

YES?
SIR, YOU'VE GOT ANOTHER ENGAGEMENT IN FIVE MINUTES.

BETSY, YOUR "BEST FRIEND" WHO IS "ON LOAN FROM GOD," WILL "WRING YOUR NECK" IF YOU'RE LATE!
©B Trudeau

SORRY— THE WIFE! GOTTA RUN!
WHAT... WHO WAS THAT? HELLO?

SO, JOSEPH! I UNDERSTAND YOU'RE STILL KILLING 'EM OUT THERE!

YEAH, TEEN SMOKING IS UP AGAIN, AND I'VE GOT A **MONSTER** SHARE OF THE CHILDREN'S MARKET.

SOMETIMES I AMAZE EVEN MYSELF! I MEAN, I DON'T EVEN EXIST, BUT MILLIONS OF KIDS THINK I'M ONE TOTALLY SLAMMIN' ROLE MODEL!

I KNOW WHAT YOU MEAN, GREAT ONE! I, TOO, AM ONLY THE FIGMENT OF AN AD-MAN'S IMAGINATION...

AND YET...
POOF!
GBTrudeau

WHAT? WHAT? I WAS TALKIN' TO SOMEONE!
STAND STILL. I'M THINKING OF RE-DRAWING YOU...

HEY... THERE'S A PRESS CONFERENCE AT JUSTICE TODAY?
YUP. WE'RE ANNOUNCING SOME INDICTMENTS.

YOU KNOW THOSE TOBACCO EXECUTIVES WHO SWORE UNDER OATH THAT SMOKING ISN'T HARMFUL? TURNS OUT THEIR **OWN** RESEARCH PROVED OTHERWISE.

SO WE'RE TALKING WHAT... PERJURY?
YUP. AND GUESS WHO'S HEADING UP THE GOVERNMENT'S TEAM.
©B Trudeau

YOU? YOU'RE TAKING DOWN THE TOBACCO LORDS?
AFTER I FINISH MY BAGEL.

GOOD MORNING, LADIES AND GENTLEMEN. MY NAME IS JOANIE CAUCUS, AND I'M AN ATTORNEY WITH THE CRIMINAL DIVISION HERE AT JUSTICE...

AS YOU CAN SEE FROM YOUR HANDOUTS, THE GOVERNMENT HAS MOVED TO INDICT SEVEN TOBACCO INDUSTRY EXECUTIVES FOR FALSELY TESTIFYING BEFORE CONGRESS.

THE INDICTMENT WAS FILED IN DISTRICT COURT THIS MORNING. ANY QUESTIONS?
MS. CAUCUS, WILL YOU BE COLLARING THESE EXECUTIVES PUBLICLY?

IF NECESSARY. BUT THERE'LL BE NO ARRESTS AT SECOND HOMES OR CLUBS.
WHAT IF THEY SEEK SANCTUARY?
©B Trudeau

LADIES AND GENTLEMEN, AS YOU CAN SEE FROM THE INDICTMENTS, THE GOVERNMENT HAS FILED IN THE U.S. DISTRICT COURT...

...CHARGING THE FOLLOWING TOBACCO EXECUTIVES, WILLIAM CAMPBELL, JAMES JOHNSTON, ANDREW TISCH, JOSEPH TADDEO, DONALD JOHNSTON, THOMAS SANDEFUR AND EDWARD HORRIGAN...

...WITH MULTIPLE COUNTS OF PERJURY AND FALSE STATEMENT IN SWORN TESTIMONY BEFORE THE U.S. CONGRESS.

BUT THEY WERE **KIDDING!** WHAT, YOU CAN'T **KID** UNDER OATH?
JOANIE, WILL THERE BE A PERP WALK WE CAN SHOOT?
©B Trudeau

WHEW... GLAD THAT'S OVER!
YOU WERE GREAT, BOSS. YOU NAILED IT!

THANKS. I JUST HOPE WE HAVEN'T OVERLOOKED ANYTHING. THE STAKES ARE SO HIGH IN THIS ONE...

JOANIE, EVEN IF IT WEREN'T A VERY STRONG CASE—WHICH IT IS—THE TOBACCO LORDS CAN'T BE VERY HAPPY WITH YOU RIGHT NOW!

YOU HEARD ME—I WANT HER DEAD!
BUT, SIRE—SHE DOESN'T SMOKE!
GB Trudeau

I CAN'T BELIEVE I'VE TAKEN THIS ON...
HOW BIG A TEAM DO WE HAVE, BOSS?

I COULD ONLY TALK JANET INTO THREE ATTORNEYS—YOU, ME AND VIC. WE GOT A LOT OF WORK AHEAD OF US...
BOY, I'LL SAY...

EXCUSE ME, BOSS, I JUST TALKED TO A SOURCE AT PHILIP MORRIS ABOUT THEIR LEGAL DEFENSE...
AND?
GB Trudeau

THEY'VE BUDGETED $4 BILLION.
WHY DO I SUDDENLY NEED A CIGARETTE?

PETER, ABC NEWS HAS LEARNED THROUGH TOUGH DIGGING THAT TOP TOBACCO COMPANY EXECUTIVES WILL BE SURRENDERING TODAY...

THE SEVEN MEN HAVE BEEN CHARGED WITH LYING UNDER OATH TO CONGRESS WHEN THEY CLAIMED SMOKING WAS NEITHER HARMFUL NOR ADDICTIVE.

WHEN THEY WILL ARRIVE IS ANYONE'S... HOLD IT! A CARAVAN OF LIMOS HAS JUST PULLED UP! THE TOBACCO LORDS HAVE ARRIVED!
GB Trudeau

NO COMMENT! NO COMMENT!
WE ALL HAVE BOOK DEALS! LET US THROUGH!

HEY, PAL, NO SMOKING IN HERE!
BUT I'M HERE TO SURRENDER! ME AND THE **LORDS OF TOBACCO!**

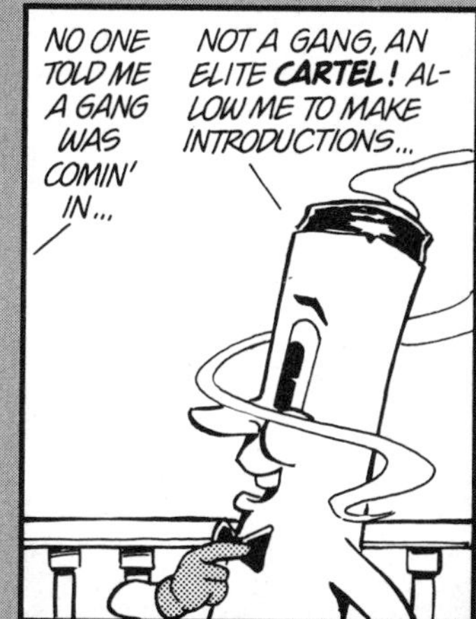
NO ONE TOLD ME A GANG WAS COMIN' IN...
NOT A GANG, AN ELITE **CARTEL!** ALLOW ME TO MAKE INTRODUCTIONS...

THIS IS **BILL CAMPBELL**, DISTINGUISHED CEO OF PHILIP MORRIS; **TOM SANDEFUR**, B&W'S MAN; **ED HORRIGAN** FROM LIGGETT; U.S. TOBACCO'S **JOE TADDEO**; **ANDY TISCH**, CEO OF LORILLARD; **JIM JOHNSTON** OF REYNOLDS; AND ATC'S CEO, **DON JOHNSTON!**

CHARMED.
SAY HELLO, BOYS.
HI.
HI.
HI.
HI.
HI.

THE CARCINOGEN SEVEN ARE BOOKED.
6'2"
6'
5'10"
5'8"
5'6"
DROP THE COAT, PLEASE!
SANDEFUR, THOMAS E.
787-35200-E
DC POLICE DEPT.

THANK YOU! **NEXT!**
THAT'S ME, RIGHT?

OKAY, GENTLEMEN, WE GOTTA TAKE YOUR PRINTS!
IS THIS A HOOT OR **WHAT?**
100mm
90mm
80mm
70mm
BUTTS, MR.
786-342718
DC POLICE DEPT.

STICK OUT YOUR FINGERS, PLEASE...
OOPS! WRONG FINGERS!
CHILL, BOYS, **CHILL!**
100mm
90mm
80mm
70mm
BUTTS, MR.
786-342718

MS. CAUCUS, THIS ARRAIGNMENT IS ALREADY RUNNING 20 MINUTES BEHIND SCHEDULE...

WILL YOU BE PRODUCING THE DEFENDANTS ANY TIME SOON?
I APOLOGIZE TO THE COURT, YOUR HONOR...

...BUT WE'VE HAD SOME UNEXPECTED DELAYS IN PROCESSING THE ARRESTS.

HEY! THIS ISN'T MY **GOOD** SIDE!
I KNOW MY RIGHTS! I **DEMAND** TO SEE MY PUBLICIST!
100mm
90mm
80mm
70mm
60mm
BUTTS, MR.
786-342718
DC POLICE DEPT.

ALL RIGHT, IN THE CASE OF THE UNITED STATES V. THE TOBACCO LORDS, HOW DO THE DEFENDANTS PLEA?

NOT GUILTY, YOUR HONOR!

A PLEA OF NOT GUILTY IS HEREBY NOTED. GIVEN THE EGREGIOUS NATURE OF THE CHARGES...

...BAIL IS SET AT $7 BILLION!
IT IS TO LAUGH! CASH OKAY?

OKAY, SO I DIDN'T PACK ENOUGH BAIL! I'M GOOD FOR IT, I TELL YA!

UH-HUH. BUT UNTIL YOU POST IT, YOU'RE OUR GUEST.
WHAT?...

YOU'RE PUTTING ME IN THE HOOSEGOW? THROWING ME IN WITH LOWLIFE SCUM?

DUDE! THEY FINALLY GOT YOU!
OH, MR. JAY! THANK GOD IT'S YOU...

IT DOESN'T FEEL LIKE 25 YEARS HAVE GONE BY SINCE WOODSTOCK, DOES IT, CORNELL?
SURE DON'T, BRO.

WE WERE SUCH CHILDREN, WEREN'T WE? SITTING OUT IN THAT SOGGY COW PASTURE, HALF NAKED, FULLY STONED, GROOVIN' ON THE VIBES OF AN ERA...

I'LL NEVER FORGET IT, MAN!
ZONKER, WHAT ARE YOU TALKING ABOUT? YOU WERE NEVER AT WOOD-STOCK.

I WASN'T?
NO. YOU ONLY SAW THE MOVIE, REMEMBER?

OH, MY GOODNESS— YOU'RE RIGHT! HOW EMBARRASSING...
MEDIA CAN MESS WITH YOUR MIND LIKE THAT, Z.
GB Trudeau

WHOA! DO YOU SUPPOSE I WASN'T AT THE MOON LANDING EITHER?
WELL, I ALWAYS THOUGHT YOU WERE A LITTLE FUZZY ON DETAIL, MAN...

JURY SELECTION STARTS IN AN HOUR, EARL. WE BETTER GET GOING...
FINE, IF WE CAN GET PAST THE PROTESTERS.

WELL, I WARNED YOU THAT MIGHT HAPPEN. THE TOBACCO INDUSTRY HAS A **LOT** OF ALLIES AROUND TOWN...

I KNOW. IT'S JUST THAT IT'S STARTING TO GET VERY UGLY AND PERSONAL OUT THERE...

LIFESTYLE **NAZIS!**
LIFESTYLE **NAZIS!**
WHAT'S **NEXT**– BEER?
UNFAIR!

MS. CAUCUS, MAY I ASK WHY YOU AND YOUR TEAM ARE SO LATE IN GETTING TO JURY SELECTION THIS MORNING?

I'M SORRY, YOUR HONOR. WE RAN INTO DEMONSTRATORS EVERYWHERE—OUTSIDE THE JUSTICE DEPARTMENT, THE COURTHOUSE, THE ELEVATOR...

WELL, FIGURE OUT A DIFFERENT ROUTE NEXT TIME, MS. CAUCUS. HOW ABOUT THE DEFENSE? ARE YOU PEOPLE READY?

SHE'S IN— CALL THEM OFF!
UH... YES, SIR! READY!

OKAY, WE'RE RUNNING LATE, BUT BEFORE SELECTION BEGINS, I HAVE A FEW WORDS FOR THE PROSPECTIVE JURORS...

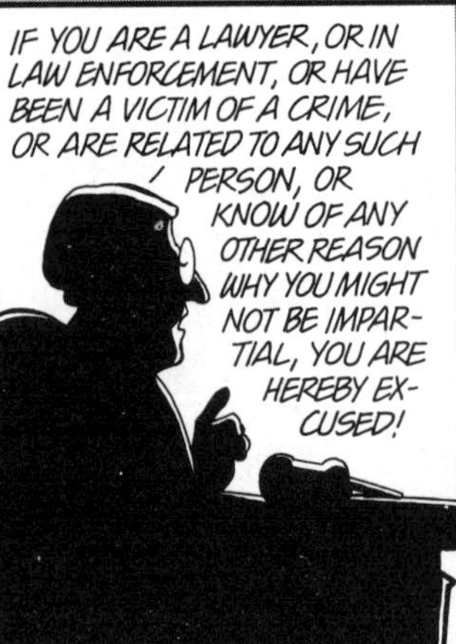
IF YOU ARE A LAWYER, OR IN LAW ENFORCEMENT, OR HAVE BEEN A VICTIM OF A CRIME, OR ARE RELATED TO ANY SUCH PERSON, OR KNOW OF ANY OTHER REASON WHY YOU MIGHT NOT BE IMPARTIAL, YOU ARE HEREBY EXCUSED!

OKAY, YOU REMAINING JURORS WILL NOW BE QUESTIONED BY THE PROSECUTOR AND THE DEFENSE ATTORNEY. EVERYONE CLEAR?

UH... NO. WHAT?
LUNCHTIME, YOUR HONOR!

MS. LUCKENBLATT, ARE YOU A PROFESSIONAL? A DECISION MAKER? DO YOU HOLD A POSITION THAT CARRIES ANY RESPONSIBILITY WHATSOEVER?

UM... NO. NOT REALLY.
ARE YOU INFORMED? EDUCATED? ARTICULATE? DO YOU HAVE ANY OPINIONS ABOUT ANYTHING? ANYTHING AT **ALL?**

WELL, I'M... I'M NOT EXACTLY SURE...
SHE'LL DO, YOUR HONOR.
GB Trudeau

WHAT, THEY ONLY ALLOW HUMAN CLAY?
DON'T WORRY, IT WORKS FOR US, TOO.

MR. JONES, HOW DO YOU FEEL ABOUT SMOKING?
I HAVE NO OPINIONS ABOUT SMOKING.

REALLY? NO OPINIONS WHATSOEVER?
NOPE. I'D BE THE PERFECT JUROR!

I SEE. MR. JONES, HAVE YOU EVER MET AN INDIVIDUAL BY THE NAME OF MR. BUTTS?
NO, NEVER! WELL, MAYBE ONCE AT A FAMILY REUNION...

AHA!
DAMN!...
GB Trudeau

MR. CAVENDISH, ARE YOU AWARE OF ANY RECENT NEWS REPORTS CONCERNING THE TOBACCO INDUSTRY AND CONGRESS?

NO, I NEVER FOLLOW THE NEWS. I DON'T READ THE PAPERS, EITHER. ONLY THE JOURNALS!
WHAT JOURNALS ARE THOSE, SIR?

PHILATELIST JOURNALS! THAT'S ALL I CARE ABOUT— STAMPS, STAMPS, STAMPS! THAT PLUS A SPECIAL LADY!
I SEE. THANK YOU, SIR.

WANT TO SEE MY COLLECTION, YOUR HONOR? I COULD INTRODUCE IT AS EVIDENCE!
HE OKAY WITH YOU?
YEAH, I'M LATE FOR LUNCH.
GB Trudeau

LADIES AND GENTLEMEN, IN THE DAYS AHEAD, THE GOVERNMENT WILL PROVE THAT SEVEN TOBACCO EXECUTIVES KNOWINGLY AND WILLFULLY LIED TO CONGRESS...

AND WE'LL PROVE **QUITE** THE OPPOSITE! GOOD LUCK TO BOTH SIDES!

THAT'S THE SPIRIT! I TIP MY HAT TO YOUR PLUCK—**AND** YOUR CRAVAT! LET THE TRIAL **BEGIN**!
©B Trudeau

THANKS, BUDDY!
HOLD IT! WHAT ABOUT THE PRE-TRIAL PUBLICITY? ANY PROBLEM?
YOUR **HONOR**!
OKAY, EVERYONE, **CHILL**!

MEMBERS OF THE JURY— LET'S REMEMBER WHAT THE EXECUTIVES REALLY **SAID**! THEY SAID THEY "**BELIEVED**" TOBACCO TO BE SAFE AND NON-ADDICTIVE!

WITH PERJURY, THE ISSUE IS **INTENT**! THE ISSUE IS WHETHER THE TOBACCO LORDS **KNEW** THEY WERE LYING!

I SUBMIT THEY **COULDN'T** HAVE KNOWN! **NO ONE** COULD LIVE WITH HIMSELF IF HE THOUGHT HE WAS PEDDLING A PRODUCT THAT KILLED MILLIONS! IT'D BE TOO MONSTROUS!
©B Trudeau

MAYBE THEY DRINK! YOU KNOW, TO FORGET!
DO THESE MEN LOOK **DRUNK**? I MEAN, AS A GROUP?

MR. SANDEFUR, ON APRIL 14, 1994, YOU SWORE UNDER OATH THAT YOU DIDN'T BELIEVE NICOTINE WAS ADDICTIVE. AND YET YOUR **OWN** COMPANY HAS PRODUCED NUMEROUS STUDIES INDICATING THE CONTRARY!

I DIDN'T KNOW ABOUT THOSE STUDIES. THEY WEREN'T CONDUCTED ON MY WATCH.
WHAT IF THEY HAD BEEN?
EXHIBIT A

THEY WOULDN'T HAVE SHAKEN MY OPINION THAT NICOTINE IS NOT ADDICTIVE.
MR. SANDEFUR, WHAT COLOR IS THE SKY?

IN MY OPINION, IT IS GREEN.
NO FURTHER QUESTIONS.
©B Trudeau

ONE LAST QUESTION, MR. SANDEFUR. IF NICOTINE IS NON-ADDICTIVE, WHY DID YOUR COMPANY DEVELOP A NEW TOBACCO STRAIN WITH TWICE THE NICOTINE OF EXISTING TOBACCOS?

THAT'S AN EASY ONE— TASTE! I'M A BEAR ABOUT CREATING TASTE!
TASTE. FUNNY HOW TASTE ISN'T MENTIONED IN ANY OF YOUR RESEARCH.

MR. SANDEFUR, DOES IT EVER CONCERN YOU THAT YOUR "OPINIONS" ABOUT NICOTINE ARE SHARED BY VIRTUALLY NO ONE IN THE WORLD BUT THE OTHER DEFENDANTS?

NO. THIS IS AMERICA. WE'RE COVERED.
GAD-ZOOKS! WHAT CHEEK!
MR. CAVEN-DISH! PLEASE!
GB Trudeau

MR. BUTTS, ON APRIL 14, 1994, YOU TOLD CONGRESS THAT YOU BELIEVED THAT SMOKING WAS SAFE, CORRECT?

SURE, BUT YOU KNOW, SAFETY ISN'T REALLY MY DEPARTMENT! I'M OUT OF THE SCIENCE LOOP! I'M JUST A GOOD-WILL AMBASSADOR!

SO YOU DON'T RECRUIT YOUNG PEOPLE TO SMOKE?
ME? HEAVENS, NO! I WOULDN'T PRESUME! SMOKING IS A DEEPLY PERSONAL CHOICE!

MR. BUTTS, WHERE WERE YOU DURING THE GULF WAR?
THAT'S DIFFERENT! THOSE KIDS WERE TRAINED TO TAKE RISKS!
GB Trudeau

BOY, THAT WITNESS DID WELL! I'M QUITE AMAZED!
YOUR HONOR!
MR. CAVEN-DISH!

ANY MORE COMMENTS FROM YOU, AND YOU WILL BE IMMEDIATELY DISMISSED FROM THE JURY! IS THAT CLEAR?
ROGER, WILCO, YOUR HONOR!

YOUR HONOR?
WHAT NOW?

REQUEST PERMISSION TO GET AN ASHTRAY!
NO, NO, I'LL BE OKAY. IT'S JUST BEEN A LONG DAY...
GB Trudeau

RUSH LIMBAUGH DOES O.J.
OKAY, FOLKS, SO IF YOU ENHANCE THE 911 TAPE, AS WE DID, IT PUTS A DIFFERENT SLANT ON THINGS...

CLEARLY, THERE'S SOME KIND OF PHILANDERING GOING ON. WE DON'T KNOW WHO OR WHEN—THE STORY KEEPS CHANGING. THERE ARE ALL KINDS OF CONTRADICTORY REPORTS...

AND IN THAT REGARD, AND I'M NOT MAKING THIS UP—GUESS WHOSE ALIBI IN THIS SORDID AFFAIR IS STARTING TO UNRAVEL...

THAT'S RIGHT, FOLKS—**HILLARY CLINTON'S!**
I **KNEW** IT! I **KNEW** SHE WAS INVOLVED!
WOW...

RUSH ON O.J.
SO WE ENHANCED THE 911 TAPE SO WE COULD MAKE OUT WHAT O.J. WAS SHOUTING...

AND, FOLKS, IT SOUNDS LIKE IT WAS A LOVE TRIANGLE KIND OF SITUATION, WHICH AT LEAST MAKES O.J.'S ANGER MORE UNDERSTANDABLE...

...EVEN THOUGH THEY WERE DIVORCED AT THE TIME. TO O.J., IT MAY HAVE BEEN LIKE WAIVERS—HE FELT HE STILL HAD AN OPTION!
GOOD ANALOGY.

SO WAS HILLARY INVOLVED? TOO SOON TO SAY!
THE MAN'S FAIR.
THANK GOODNESS!

MY FRIENDS, DIDN'T YOU JUST **KNOW** THE FEMINAZIS WOULD TAKE THE O.J. FOOTBALL AND RUN WITH IT?

DOMESTIC **ABUSE!** THAT'S ALL WE HEAR ABOUT NOW, THANKS TO THEIR SOCIALIST UTOPIAN FRIENDS IN THE MEDIA...

HOW MUCH "ABUSE" IS THERE, REALLY? VIRTUALLY NONE! STUDIES SHOW WOMEN ARE **24** TIMES MORE LIKELY TO BE STRUCK BY LIGHTNING THAN BY AN EX-FOOTBALL STAR!

I'M NOT MAKING THIS UP, FOLKS! I COULD **NOT** MAKE THIS UP!
NO NEED TO! IT'S ALL THERE!

FOLKS, SOME OF YOU MAY HAVE BEEN HEARING THAT PRINCE CHARLES RECENTLY DECIDED TO ADD INFIDELITY TO HIS PERMANENT RECORD!

WHY, MY FRIENDS, CAN'T ANYONE IN THE HOUSE O'WINDSOR KEEP HIS PANTS ON? AND WHY ON EARTH DO THEY TALK ABOUT IT?

AND WHO WAS THE LUCKY ADULTERESS, YOU ASK? WELL, WHO DO YOU SUPPOSE WAS SEEN ENTERING THE PALACE THROUGH THE **FRONT** ENTRANCE THIS SPRING? I'M NOT MAKING THIS UP...

THAT'S RIGHT- **HILLARY!**
FIGURES.
BOY, SHE'S GOT A BUSY SCHEDULE!

DID YOU SEE HOW CLINTON IS AFTER ME AGAIN? FOLKS, DON'T YOU THINK THE PRESIDENT WOULD HAVE BETTER THINGS TO DO WITH HIS TIME?

YOU KNOW WHO STARTED ALL THOSE JOKES ABOUT ME, DON'T YOU...?
WHAT JOKES? YOU HEARD ANY?
SURE!...

PAID WHITE HOUSE STAFF, **THAT'S** WHO!
WHAT'S THE DIFFERENCE BETWEEN LIMBAUGH AND THE "HINDENBURG"?

YOUR TAX DOLLARS AT WORK!
I GIVE UP.
ONE'S A FLAMING NAZI GASBAG; THE OTHER'S JUST A DIRIGIBLE.

MY FRIENDS, RECENTLY THE FEMINAZIS AND WACKOS AT "FAIR" ISSUED A REPORT QUESTIONING THE ACCURACY OF SOME OF MY STATEMENTS. WHY? BECAUSE THEY **RESENT** THE STRAIGHT TALK ON MY SHOWS!

WHO ELSE HAS HAD THE GUTS TO TALK ABOUT VINT FOSTER'S 1992 MURDER IN ROOSEVELT PARK ONLY **DAYS** AFTER THE F.B.I. SUBPOENAED HIS WHITEWATER FILES AND TAPES?

WHO ELSE WOULD BREAK THE STORY OF CHELSEA'S 7TH GRADE PAPER, "WHY I FEEL GUILTY BEING WHITE," THE **SAME DAY** CONGRESS VOTED AGAINST THE GULF WAR TO KEEP BUSH FROM BEING DEFEATED IN 1990?
NO **WONDER** I SCARE THEM!

HEY, KIDS! CAN **YOU** SPOT RUSH'S **BIG LIES!** THERE ARE **TEN** IN ALL!
IT'S EASY... **AND** EDUCATIONAL! **HAVE FUN!**

HI, EVERYBODY! IT'S THAT TIME AGAIN — **SUMMER RERUNS!**
SO SIT BACK AND ENJOY THIS **FAVORITE** STRIP FROM THE PAST!

ZONKER'S BIG NEWS.
PARIS? YOU'RE OFF TO **PARIS?**
I SAIL TUESDAY NEXT!

WHAT ON EARTH FOR, SPORT?
EVERYONE'S DOING IT! EX-PAT ALIENATION AND ALL THAT! I HEAR THERE'S A GRAND CROWD GADDING ABOUT IN MONTMARTRE!

BUT HOW WILL YOU KEEP BODY AND SOUL TOGETHER?
GRANDFATHER LEFT ME A SPOT OF STOCK! TRUTH BE TOLD, I'M SITTING RATHER PRETTY!

GAD, ZONK! YOU'RE QUITE THE ODD DUCK, AREN'T YOU? PARIS, INDEED.
HEY, MEN! ANY OF YOU OWN STOCK?
CRASH!

UM... A LITTLE DATED, ISN'T IT?
NAH, PEOPLE **LOVE** THIS OLD STUFF!
HEE, HEE! CHECK OUT YOUR HAIR!
GBTrudeau

I'M SORRY, RAY, B.D.'S NOT HERE. HE'S IN TOWN TAKING A MEETING WITH SID...
COOL. YOU GOT A NEW GIG?

NO, IT'S NOT ABOUT ME. SID'S HELPING HIM COORDINATE SOME INTERVIEWS...

B.D. WAS INVOLVED IN THE O.J. SIMPSON FREEWAY CHASE, AND NOW HE'S BEING BESIEGED WITH OFFERS TO TELL HIS EXCLUSIVE STORY!

OPRAH? SID! MY CLIENT LOVED THE FLOWERS, BABE! LOVED THEM!
SURE I DID. GET THE BOTTOM LINE.

OKAY, B.D., LET ME LAY THIS OUT FOR YOU. YOU'RE SITTING ON A GREAT STORY HERE. YOU WERE THE ONLY COP TO GET CLOSE TO THE BRONCO DURING THE CHASE...

YOU'VE GOT TWO CHOICES. YOU CAN EITHER TAKE THE HIGH ROAD, GO TO THE NETWORKS, AND TALK TO ANYONE FOR FREE...

OR?
OR WE MARKET AN EXCLUSIVE INTERVIEW TO TABLOID TELEVISION FOR A HUMONGOUS PILE OF MONEY.

I DON'T UNDERSTAND. WHY ARE WE HAVING THIS DISCUSSION?
FINE! JUST SO LONG AS WE'RE ON THE SAME WAVELENGTH.

I WANT YOU TO GO FOR IT WITH MY STORY, SID! TOP DOLLAR, BIDDING WARS, THE WHOLE NINE YARDS!
YOU GOT IT, CHIEF!

WHAT DO YOU THINK THE INTERVIEW'S WORTH? 50 GRAND? 100?
WELL, I... HEY... I JUST REALIZED SOMETHING—YOU'RE A COP!

WELL, OF COURSE I'M A COP. SO WHAT?
SO YOU'RE NOT ALLOWED TO TALK! YOU'RE A MATERIAL WITNESS! YOU MIGHT HAVE TO TESTIFY, AND YOU CAN'T BE TAINTED!

BUT I DIDN'T SEE ANYTHING! NOTHING!
HOLD IT...

I'D GRAB THIS ONE UP, KIDDO! I CALLED YOU FIRST BECAUSE I OWE YOU ONE, BUT I CAN'T KEEP "HARD COPY" ON HOLD FOR-EVER!
B.D. WAS ON THE SCENE, UP CLOSE AND PERSONAL! HE WAS PART OF O.J.'S POLICE ESCORT THE WHOLE WAY HOME!
I DUNNO, SID. IT DOESN'T SOUND THAT PRO-MISING...
UH-HUH. AND WHAT IF I WERE TO TELL YOU THAT MY CLIENT SAW THE JUICE HIDE A 15-INCH KNIFE UN-DER THE BACK SEAT OF THE BRONCO?

HE DID?
WHO KNOWS? BUT HE WAS IN A **POSITION** TO! INTERESTED?

SORRY, B.D., COULDN'T GET A NIBBLE—EVEN FROM GERALDO. I THINK IT'S TOO MUCH O.J. MARKET SATUR-ATION.

DAMN... WHAT DO WE DO NOW?
I'D GO TO THE NON-PAYING MEDIA OUTLETS. AT LEAST YOU'LL GET SOME GOOD EXPOSURE.

CAN YOU HANDLE THAT FOR ME?
SORRY, CHIEF, I'M AN AGENT. 10% OF NADA MEANS ADIOS. WHAT YOU NEED IS A LAWYER.

A LAWYER? HOW DO I FIND A...
YOU'RE IN MALIBU. WAVE A CHECK FROM YOUR WINDOW.

WHAT IS IT, B.D.? WHAT'S THE EMERGENCY?
I'VE GOT A REPRE-SENTATION CRISIS, JOANIE...

I WAS A PARTICIPANT IN THE O.J. FREEWAY CHASE, BUT WE CAN'T GET ANY OF THE TABS TO BUY THE RIGHTS. SID SAYS I NEED A LAWYER TO SHOP ME TO THE NON-PAYING MEDIA.

THAT'S IT? THAT'S WHAT YOU CALLED ME ABOUT?
WHAT, LIKE YOU'RE DOING SOMETHING MORE IMPORTANT RIGHT NOW?

HECK, **NO**, B.D.! I'LL JUST DROP EVERY-THING!
HEY, COULD YOU HURRY IT UP? THE JUDGE IS GETTING STEAMED!

LOOK AT THAT SMUG FACE...

YOU'D THINK THEY'D AL-READY WON AN ACQUITTAL!
HEY, YOU DID GREAT, JOANIE— DON'T WORRY ABOUT HIM.

THERE'S NO WAY THAT THAT JURY ISN'T COMING BACK IN WITH GUILTY VERDICTS! NO WAY!

INNOCENT! HOW COULD YOU THINK THEY'RE INNOCENT?
INSTINCT! I JUST LIKED THE CUT OF THEIR JIBS!

HEY, C'MON, JEREMY, THIS IS A NO-BRAINER. ALL THE REST OF US ARE VOTING TO CON-VICT. WHAT'S THE PROBLEM?

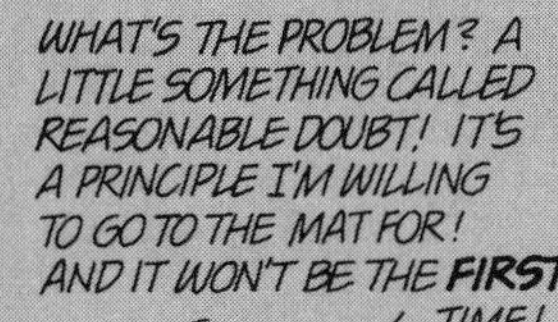
WHAT'S THE PROBLEM? A LITTLE SOMETHING CALLED REASONABLE DOUBT! IT'S A PRINCIPLE I'M WILLING TO GO TO THE MAT FOR! AND IT WON'T BE THE FIRST TIME!

I'LL NEVER FORGET MY FIRST ORNITHOLOGICAL NOMENCLA-TURE CONVENTION! A BIRDER FROM OREGON INSISTED HE'D DISCOVERED A NEW LOON! THE EVIDENCE WAS SCANT! I VOTED NAY! AN UPROAR ENSUED!

CAN ANYONE HERE DO A LOON? I CAN! PHWOO!
OOPS... THAT'S AN EGRET...
TELL THE JUDGE WE HAVE A SITUATION.

OKAY, IT LOOKS LIKE JEREMY HERE IS THE ONLY HOLDOUT AGAINST A GUILTY VERDICT...

I PROPOSE WE WORK ON HIM IN TEAMS. YOU THREE PRESENT THE LEGAL ARGUMENTS, AND YOU TWO GUYS ON THE END RESTATE THE MORAL CASE FOR CONVICTION...

THE REST OF US WILL ARGUE FROM A COMMONSENSE PERSPECTIVE. WE'LL ROTATE THE TEAMS. IF YOU FEEL TIRED, LET A TEAMMATE TAKE OVER. WITH LUCK, WE'LL WEAR HIM DOWN BY TONIGHT. GOOD LUCK!

SORRY FOR ALL THE TROUBLE.
NO PROBLEM. YOU'D DO IT FOR US.

WE LOOK FORWARD TO A LONG, DRAWN-OUT APPELLATE PROCESS THAT MAY WELL DRAG ON **YEARS** AFTER ALL THE PRINCIPALS ARE DEAD! THANK YOU!

HELLO?
MRS. D? JEREMY HERE! I'VE JUST HAD THE MOST REMARKABLE EXPERIENCE! SHALL WE HAVE DINNER SO I CAN BRING YOU UP TO SPEED?

WELL, I DON'T KNOW, DEAR. DO YOU THINK WE COULD KEEP IT LIGHT? JUST GET TOGETHER AS OLD FRIENDS?
I WOULD **INSIST** ON IT, MRS. D!

VERY WELL, THEN, DEAR, I ACCEPT.
HOLD IT! WHAT IF WE HIT IT OFF LIKE GANGBUSTERS AND A MARRIAGE PROPOSAL JUST **POPS** OUT?

THAT WOULD BE A PROBLEM FOR ME, DEAR.
SAME HERE! I'M STILL PLAYING THE FIELD!
GB Trudeau

SO WHAT WAS YOUR BIG ADVENTURE, JEREMY DEAR?
JURY SERVICE, MRS. D! THREE WEEKS OF IT!

AT FIRST, I WASN'T SURE I'D BE PICKED! ALL SORTS OF PEOPLE SHOWED UP, BUT ONLY A SELECT FEW— AN ELITE, IF YOU WILL— MADE THE CUT!

THE LAWYERS FOR BOTH SIDES INTERVIEWED US, ASKING US POINTED QUESTIONS, SOME OF THEM **QUITE** PERSONAL! I EVEN HAD TO TELL THEM ABOUT US!

"US," JEREMY?
I HAD NO CHOICE, MRS. D! THEY **GRILLED** ME!
GB Trudeau

LET ME RECREATE THE DRAMA OF THE JURY ROOM FOR YOU, MRS. D! I HOPE I CAN DO IT JUSTICE!
I'M SURE YOU CAN, DEAR..

AT FIRST, IT SEEMED CUT AND DRIED! AFTER ALL, THESE GUYS WERE TOBACCO EXECUTIVES! PARIAHS! CASE CLOSED!
BUT THEN I THOUGHT, HOLD ON! THEY'RE NOT TOBACCO EXECUTIVES, THEY'RE **HUMAN BEINGS!**

THEY HAVE FAMILIES AND FRIENDS! THEY HAVE FEELINGS AND DREAMS JUST LIKE **OTHER** HUMAN BEINGS!
GB Trudeau

BUT THEN I THOUGHT, HOLD ON! THEY'RE NOT HUMAN BEINGS— THEY'RE **TOBACCO EXECUTIVES!**
HEAVENS! WHAT A PICKLE!

ANYWAY, I WASN'T SURE THAT THE STATE HAD PROVEN ITS CASE! SO I SAID SO!

MY FELLOW JURORS WERE THUNDERSTRUCK! THEY HADN'T ANTICIPATED MY PRINCIPLED STAND AGAINST POLITICAL CORRECTNESS.

OH, THE FRAY THAT FOLLOWED! IT WAS TO AND FRO THROUGH THE NIGHT! I STUCK TO MY GUNS AS LONG AS I COULD, BUT FINALLY I WAS FORCED TO CAPITULATE! DON'T ASK WHY!

I WON'T, DEAR.
I REALLY, REALLY, REALLY NEEDED TO USE THE FACILITIES!
GB Trudeau

JEREMY, I'M **VERY** IMPRESSED BY YOUR CHOICE OF RESTAURANTS! WAS IT DIFFICULT TO GET A RESERVATION?

WELL, INITIALLY. JACQUES AND I HAVE A BIT OF A HISTORY. WHEN I CALLED TO BOOK A TABLE, HE ASKED, "WHO'S PAYING?"

GOODNESS! THAT SEEMS A LITTLE TACKY...
THAT'S WHAT **I** THOUGHT! I WAS SO IRATE, I GAVE HIM YOUR NAME!

YOU WHAT?
THE CHECK, MADAM.
SHH! PLAY ALONG! WE'LL LOSE FACE...
GB Trudeau

JEREMY CAVENDISH! HOW COULD YOU?
SORRY YOU HAD TO PICK UP THE CHECK FOR DINNER, MRS. D...

I JUST COULDN'T GIVE JACQUES THE SATISFACTION OF REFUSING MY BUSINESS! HERE—I'M MAKING AMENDS IMMEDIATELY! THIS IS FOR THE FULL AMOUNT, PLUS INTEREST AND HANDLING CHARGES!
RIPP!

WHO CARES IF MY ANNUITY FROM UNCLE MORT'S TRUST IS ALWAYS A LITTLE LATE IN ARRIVING? A DEBT IS A DEBT! ONE MUST STEP UP MANFULLY TO ONE'S OBLIGATIONS!

YOU JUST WROTE ME A BAD CHECK, DIDN'T YOU?
AS A JOKE! I WAS GOING TO WIRE YOU THE REAL MONEY IN THE MORNING!
GB Trudeau

MONDAY.
TIME TO GO TO SCHOOL, HON...
OKAY, MOM.

I JUST GOTTA GET MY HOMEWORK. THANKS FOR CHECKING IT FOR ME, BY THE WAY...
Milk

I'LL BE DOWN IN A FLASH. I KNOW YOU'VE BOTH GOT TO GET TO WORK...

COMING ALONG NICELY, ISN'T HE?
WELL, YEAH. IT'S SORT OF INCREDIBLE...

I NEVER IMAGINED 12 COULD BE SUCH A CHARMING AGE.

TUESDAY.
TIME TO GO TO SCHOOL, HON...
WHY? BECAUSE YOU SAY SO? I DON'T THINK SO.

...AND AS 250,000 HAPPY CAMPERS STREAM HOME FROM WOODSTOCK II, ALL THIS REPORTER CAN SAY IS, "WOW!"
RIGHT. WHAT A NON-EVENT!

I'LL SAY! COULDN'T **TOUCH** THE ORIGINAL!
HOW WOULD **YOU** KNOW, ZONKER? YOU ONLY RENTED THE MOVIE!

YEAH, BUT HE **COULD** HAVE BEEN AT WOODSTOCK, B.D.! IN ANOTHER LIFE — A **PARALLEL** LIFE! AS A STAR-TRAVELER TO A MAGIC REALM!
WELL, EXACTLY.

HEY, MAN, WANNA GO LIE IN A SWAMP FOR THREE DAYS?
COSMIC! WHAT? DID I SAY SOMETHING?
©B Trudeau

ZONKER, IN AN ALTERNATE ALTERNATIVE LIFETIME.
HOW MUCH FURTHER TO WOODSTOCK, MAN?
CAN'T BE TOO FAR. I CAN SMELL THE COWS.

OH, NO!... WE GOTTA GO BACK, MAN...
WHAT? WHY?

I FORGOT TO BRING MY STASH! IT **COMPLETELY** SLIPPED MY MIND!
WELL, IT'S TOO LATE, MAN. THE CONCERT STARTS IN TWO HOURS.
©B Trudeau

BUMMER. I'LL BET NO ONE ELSE REMEMBERS, EITHER.
MAYBE THEY'LL SELL BEER.

DURING A PARALLEL LIFETIME, ZONKER GOES TO WOODSTOCK.
SORRY, FOLKS — NO TICKETS, NO ENTRANCE!

BUT WE DIDN'T THINK WE **NEEDED** TICKETS, MAN! ROCK 'N' ROLL BELONGS TO THE **PEOPLE!**
SORRY.

HEY, C'MON, MAN, HAVE A HEART! WE JUST DROVE 250 MILES — AND THEN HAD TO **WALK** IN ANOTHER FIVE!
WELL... HOW MANY ARE YOU, MAN?
©B Trudeau

UM... WE'RE ABOUT A HALF MILLION STRONG.
WELL, OKAY, BUT **NOBODY** ELSE AFTER YOU FOLKS!

OH, WOW, LOOK AT THAT! FUTURE LEGEND, MAN! HENDRIX IS PLAYING GUITAR WITH HIS **TEETH!**

I WONDER IF THAT WORKS ON PLAQUE... OH, BY THE WAY, MARK...
YEAH, MAN?

I HAVE SOMETHING I'D LIKE TO SHARE WITH YOU...
BEAUTIFUL, MAN. LAY IT ON ME.

I'M HAVING MY DOUBTS ABOUT THIS ACID.
HEAVY— WE BETTER GET YOU OVER TO THE BUMMER TENT!

ZONK IS RUSHED TO THE WOODSTOCK BUMMER TENT.
IS HE GOING TO BE OKAY, MAN?
HOW MANY FINGERS, MAN?
18.

DO YOU FEEL LIKE FLYING FROM THE LIGHT TOWERS? ARE YOU BEING FOLLOWED BY THE FBI? DO YOU THINK THE COWSILLS ARE A GREAT BAND?
NO... NO, NOT YET...

HE'LL BE OKAY... HEY, JASPER! LET'S GET THIS KID OVER TO THE HOLDING TENT!

WHAT IS THIS, ACID TRIAGE?
WE'RE A LITTLE SHORT-HANDED, MAN.
MOM?

BRRING! BRRING!
OH, WOW... WHAT'S THAT RINGING, MAN?
THAT'S A WAKE-UP CALL, MAN! FOR AN ENTIRE GENERATION!

BRRING!
IT'S TELLING US WE HAVE TO LIVE WITH THE CONSEQUENCES OF WHAT WE DO HERE TODAY—THAT WOODSTOCK WILL BECOME THE TEMPLATE FOR ALL THAT FOLLOWS!

BRIING!
FAR **OUT!** WHAT ARE YOU, MAN, SOME KIND OF VISIONARY?
NO, NO... I'M JUST AN ORDINARY TOON, SENT BACK FROM THE FUTURE.

ZONKER? PHONE!
BY THE WAY, THE BEATLES ARE BREAKING UP NEXT YEAR...

HI! IT'S BARBARA ANN BOOPSTEIN FOR THE STAY-YOUNG SKIN CARE SYSTEM!

YOU KNOW, A LOT OF MY FANS HAVE COME UP TO ME AND SAID, "MS. BOOPSTEIN, WE NEVER THOUGHT WE'D SEE YOU DOING AN INFOMERCIAL! WHAT'S GOING ON?"

WELL, THE ANSWER'S VERY SIMPLE—I **LOVE** THIS PRODUCT LINE! STAY-YOUNG SKIN CARE MEANS I CAN PLAY 26 **WELL** INTO MY EARLY 30'S! AND **YOU** CAN TOO!

IF YOU DON'T MIND HAVING YOUR FLESH SEARED OFF YOUR SKULL! HISSS!

OOPS... DID WE JUST HAVE A LITTLE VISIT FROM OUR ANCIENT FRIEND?
GB Trudeau

WHAT THE HELL WAS **THAT?**
SOME GUY SHE CHANNELS FOR. DON'T WORRY—THE VIEWERS LOVE HIM.

I MEAN, HEY, I REALLY MEAN THIS ONE, THAT FROM THE HEART IN THE SENSE THAT SOME THINGS AT LEAST THE WAY I LOOK AT IT!
ME, TOO! ME, TOO! I'M **READY!**

HI, FOLKS! REMEMBER OUR POLITICAL ICONS, THOSE LITTLE BITS OF CARTOON HAIKU?
WELL, IT'S TIME TO COOK ONE UP FOR THE CURRENT WHITE HOUSE OCCUPANT...

AFTER WATCHING HIM IN ACTION SINCE TAKING OFFICE, READERS HAVE WRITTEN IN WITH ALL SORTS OF SUGGESTIONS...
LIKE A CHEESE-BURGER, OR A WIND SOCK, OR A CHICKEN LEG, OR A PADDLE, OR A KALEIDOSCOPE...

OUR TWO FAVORITES, THOUGH, COME FROM ON-LINE READERS, PROPEL-LERHEADS, WHO **KNOW** FROM ICONS!
BUT WE NEED **YOUR** HELP TO PICK THE WINNER!

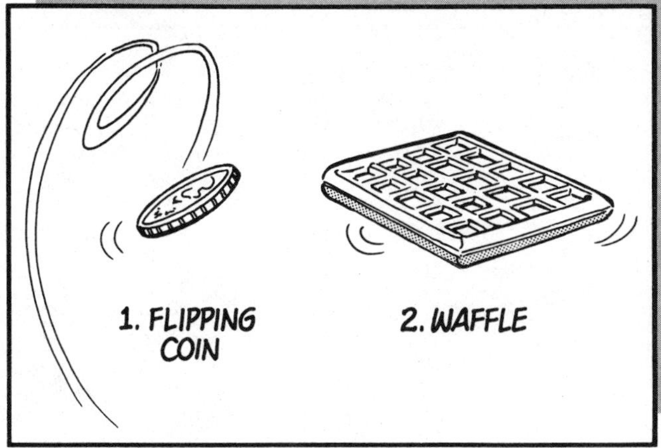
1. FLIPPING COIN
2. WAFFLE

SO LET US KNOW YOUR PREFERENCE— WE'RE RARIN' TO ACHIEVE CONSENSUS!
THAT'S RIGHT! AND IN THE SPIRIT OF THIS ADMINI-STRATION, WE COULD GO **EITHER WAY!**
GB Trudeau

HI, FOLKS! REMEMBER THE NATIONWIDE REFERENDUM WE ANNOUNCED A WEEK AGO TO SELECT A NEW PRESIDENTIAL **ICON?**

"WE ASKED READERS TO CHOOSE BETWEEN THESE TWO FINALISTS..."
1. Flipping Coin
2. Waffle

WELL, THE READERS HAVE SPOKEN — WITH A **ROAR!** SO WITHOUT ANY FURTHER ADO WHATSOEVER, HERE'S...

"... THE **PEOPLE'S CHOICE!**"
UNIVERSAL COVERAGE OR **NOTHING!**
OKAY, 90%!
I CAN LIVE WITH 70%...

THE NEW ICON GETS BUSY.
SO GIVE ME YOUR EVALUATION OF THE WHITEWATER HEARINGS SO FAR, JOSH...

WELL, SIR, I'D SAY WE TOOK A PRETTY HARD HIT. WHAT WITH THE DOZENS OF CONTRADICTIONS, DENIALS AND OBFUSCATIONS, IT'S PRETTY CLEAR WE'VE BEEN INVOLVED IN A MASSIVE COVER-UP!

IN THAT REGARD, THE STAFF HAS PRESSED ME TO ASK YOU SOMETHING, SIR...
YES?

WHAT EXACTLY ARE WE COVERING UP?
DEPENDS. WHAT ARE THE OPTIONS?

MR. PRESIDENT, I THINK I SPEAK FOR **ALL** OF US INVOLVED IN THE WHITEWATER COVER-UP...

... IN TELLING YOU THAT IT WOULD BE VERY HELPFUL TO KNOW WHAT WE'RE COVERING UP.
WHY?

WELL, IT WOULD ENABLE US TO BETTER CO-ORDINATE OUR EFFORTS.
SORRY. NO CAN DO.

CAN'T YOU EVEN TELL US IF IT'S JUICY?
IT HAS THE APPEARANCE OF JUICINESS, YES.

YOU REALLY WANT TO KNOW WHAT HAPPENED WITH WHITEWATER ALL THOSE YEARS AGO, JOSH? DO YOU?

IT MIGHT BE HELPFUL, SIR.
WELL, BASICALLY, IT BOILS DOWN TO THIS...

UH-OH! ROGUE ACID FLASHBACK!
WOW! WOW! WOW! WOW! WOW! WOW! WOW!

YOU WHAT, SIR?
TRY TO UNDERSTAND— THIS WAS ARKANSAS.

...MR. CLINTON IS NOW APPROACHING THE PODIUM. HE IS EXPECTED TO SPEAK TONIGHT ON THE SUBJECT OF WHITEWATER...
ABOUT TIME!

...AND NOW, THE PRESIDENT OF THE UNITED STATES!
MY FELLOW AMERICANS.

OH, MY GOD... LOOK!
WHAT? WHAT?

HE'S... HE'S RECUSING HIMSELF!
OH, GROSS. DOES THAT HURT?

THIS IS ROLAND HEDLEY. TODAY, DURING A LIVE PRESS CONFERENCE ON WHITEWATER, THE PRESIDENT UNEXPECTEDLY RECUSED HIMSELF!

WHITE HOUSE DOCTORS SAY MR. CLINTON SUFFERED NO ILL EFFECTS, AND THE PRESIDENT IMMEDIATELY RETURNED TO THE OVAL OFFICE!

WITH WHITEWATER AT LEAST TEMPORARILY BEHIND HIM, MR. CLINTON SPENT THE REMAINDER OF THE DAY WITH SECRETARY CHRISTOPHER CONDUCTING FOREIGN POLICY!

LET'S INVADE HAITI!
LET'S NOT!
LET'S BOMB THE SERBS!
LET'S NOT!
LET'S NOT!
LET'S HELP RWANDA!

IF ONLY...
IF ONLY...

HI, KIDS! RECOGNIZE THAT FARAWAY LOOK? YES, IT'S TIME AGAIN FOR **MIKE'S SUMMERTIME FANTASY**!

THIS YEAR'S, HOWEVER, IS NOT QUITE THE CONFECTION AS LAST YEAR'S. NO, THIS TIME AROUND, MIKE DREAMS OF **SAVING THE WORLD!** LET'S WISH HIM LUCK!

WOW... WHAT A **SENSITIVE** RE-DRAWING OF BOSNIA'S MAP!
WELL, YOU SEEMED A LITTLE STUCK, SIR.

MIKE'S SUMMER FANTASY HAS HIM SAVING THE WORLD.
GOOD NEWS, MIKE! ALL PARTIES HAVE AGREED TO YOUR PROPOSED PARTITION OF BOSNIA!
THAT'S GREAT, SIR! OH, I'VE PREPARED SOMETHING ELSE FOR YOU.

WHAT'S THIS? WHY, IT'S A WHITE PAPER ON **HAITI!** AND IT, TOO, IS **BRILLIANT!**
I HOPE IT'LL PROVE USEFUL TO YOU, SIR! WELL, I'M OFF!

WHAT? WHERE ARE YOU GOING, MIKE?
TO SARAJEVO, MR. PRESIDENT! TO SUPERVISE THE WAR CRIME TRIALS!

THE NEXT DAY.
CONGRATULATIONS, SIR! THEY ALL PLED GUILTY!
EXCELLENT! WELL, OFF TO RWANDA!

MIKE IS SUPERVISING FREE 'N' FAIR ELECTIONS IN KIGALI.
THAT'S RIGHT, MA'AM—EVEN HUTU MAY VOTE!
SPECIAL ENVOY DOONESBURY! YOU HAVE A CALL!
DISTRICT 14

DOONESBURY HERE!
MIKE! THIS IS YOUR PRESIDENT! I NEED YOU TO HELP ME WITH CONGRESS!

BUT MR. PRESIDENT! I'M BUSY CREATING A VIABLE MODEL FOR DEMOCRATIC REFORM THROUGHOUT THE AFRICAN CONTINENT!
SORRY, MIKE! WE'VE GOT CRISES ENOUGH RIGHT HERE AT HOME! SEE YOU SOON!

HAVE TO GO, OLD FRIEND! REMEMBER— ONE PERSON, ONE VOTE, GOT IT?
GOT IT, SIR! THANKS FOR ROLLING BACK CENTURIES OF HATRED!

MIKE'S SUMMERTIME FANTASY HAS TAKEN HIM TO THE HILL.
HMM... HOW TO ASSUAGE CRITICS OF THIS CRIME BILL WITHOUT COMPROMISING THE FRAMERS' INTENT!

LET'S SEE... A SMALL CHANGE IN LANGUAGE HERE... A CLARIFICATION THERE... A CONCESSION HERE... A FEW "T"S CROSSED...

...ET VOILA!
GOOD GOD! HE'S BROKEN THE DEADLOCK!
THAT BILL WILL WIN PASSAGE IN A HEARTBEAT!
GB Trudeau

NOW, THEN! I UNDERSTAND HEALTH CARE IS STALLED...
QUICK! SOMEBODY ROUND UP ALL THE DRAFTS!

MIKE, THIS COMPREHENSIVE HEALTH CARE BILL YOU HAMMERED OUT IS ASTONISHING! NO WONDER IT RECEIVED INSTANT BIPARTISAN SUPPORT IN BOTH HOUSES!

YOU HAVE A REMARKABLE TALENT FOR BRINGING PEOPLE TOGETHER!
WELL, THANKS, SIR, BUT I WAS REALLY ONLY ACTING AT YOUR BEHEST...

IT'S NOT LIKE I'D DESERVE TO RECEIVE THE MEDAL OF FREEDOM, OUR NATION'S HIGHEST HONOR, MAKING ME THE YOUNGEST RECIPIENT IN HISTORY.

LATER THAT DAY.
CONGRATULATIONS, MIKE.
I'M NOT WORTHY, SIR. I'M TOO YOUNG.
GB Trudeau

CONGRATULATIONS ON BECOMING OUR NATION'S YOUNGEST-EVER RECIPIENT OF THE FREEDOM MEDAL, MIKE!
THANKS VERY MUCH, MRS. CLINTON.

I DON'T KNOW HOW YOU MANAGED TO SOLVE ALL OUR NATION'S PROBLEMS SO QUICKLY!
I COULDN'T HAVE DONE IT WITHOUT YOUR HUSBAND'S SUPPORT, MRS. C!

BEYOND THAT, ALL IT REALLY TOOK WAS A LITTLE COMMON SENSE AND IMAGINATION!
GB Trudeau

ESPECIALLY IMAGINATION.
THANKS, HILL. MAY I CALL YOU HILL?

*as documented by Fairness & Accuracy in Reporting

WOW, HONEY... YOU WON ALL THESE AT CAMP?
UH-HUH...

I GOT THIS ONE FOR SHOWING UP AT CAMP ON THE RIGHT DAY...

...AND THIS ONE FOR FINISHING A LANYARD. THE CUP I WAS AWARDED FOR REMEMBERING MY COMPUTER PASSWORD...

...AND THIS ONE I GOT FOR NOT MISSING TOO MANY ARCHERY PRACTICES!

UM... WELL! YOU MUST BE VERY PROUD, JEFF.
YEAH, RIGHT, MOM.

WHO KNEW IT WAS A SELF-ESTEEM CAMP?
WE GOTTA READ THE BROCHURES MORE CARE-FULLY.
GB Trudeau

TO WHAT DO I OWE THE PLEASURE, DEAN RUMPLEMEYER?
SIR, IT'S ABOUT THE REMEDIAL COURSES...

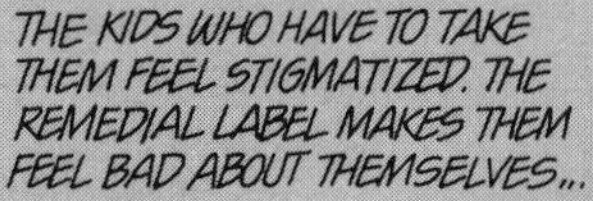
THE KIDS WHO HAVE TO TAKE THEM FEEL STIGMATIZED. THE REMEDIAL LABEL MAKES THEM FEEL BAD ABOUT THEMSELVES...

I WAS WONDERING IF WE COULD RE-NAME THEM "INTRODUCTORY" COURSES. REMEDIAL ENGLISH, FOR EXAMPLE, WOULD BECOME ENGLISH 101. AND ENGLISH 101 THEN BECOMES 201, AND SO FORTH.

YOU MEAN, **COURSE** INFLATION?
YOU MAKE IT SOUND UGLY, SIR. THESE KIDS ARE IN PAIN!

YOU WANTED TO SEE ME, SIR?
YES, CAMPBELL. DEAN RUMPLEMEYER WAS JUST IN HERE. SHE WANTS TO DE-STIGMATIZE THE REMEDIAL COURSES BY CALLING THEM "INTRODUCTORY."

WELL, SIR, THEY PRACTICALLY ALREADY ARE INTRODUCTORY COURSES. ALMOST TWO THIRDS OF THE INCOMING FRESHMEN ARE TAKING THEM...
WHAT?

ADMISSIONS SAYS IT'S GETTING HARDER AND HARDER TO ATTRACT KIDS WHO ARE PREPARED. YOU SHOULD GO TO THE FRESHMAN MEET 'N' GREET TODAY. IT'S A REAL EYE-OPENER!

REALLY? HOWARD STERN IS **MY** FAVORITE WRITER, TOO!
ALL THE OTHERS SUCK, MAN!

WELCOME TO WALDEN, SON!
THANK YOU, SIR. GOOD TO BE HERE!

PICKED YOUR COURSES YET?
YES, SIR! I'M IN REMEDIAL MATH, REMEDIAL HISTORY, REMEDIAL BIOLOGY, AND PRE-REMEDIAL ENGLISH!

WELL, GOOD LUCK TO YOU, SON.
THANK YOU, SIR! YOU, TOO!

IT'S FINALLY HAPPENED — I'M RUNNING A HIGH SCHOOL.
BUT A DAMN FINE ONE, SIR!

SO WHAT MADE YOU CHOOSE WALDEN, SON?
WELL, I WANTED A QUALITY EDUCATION, SIR...

I WENT TO A SELF-ESTEEM ACADEMY IN CALIFORNIA, AND FRANKLY, I WAS A LITTLE UNDERCHALLENGED...

I FIGURED IT WAS TIME TO PUSH MYSELF, FIND AN ELITE, HIGHLY COMPETITIVE COLLEGE WHERE I COULD REALLY PURSUE MY ACADEMIC INTERESTS!
©B Trudeau

GREAT! LIKE WHAT?
WELL, LIKE, I'M TOTALLY INTERESTED IN LEARNING HOW TO READ.

YOU KNOW, MR. PRESIDENT, THAT THING YOU SAID ABOUT RUNNING A HIGH SCHOOL STRUCK A CHORD WITH ME...

WALDEN IS GETTING KILLED IN THE MARKETPLACE. THE LOWER WE'VE SET THE BAR TO ATTRACT STUDENTS, THE MORE OUR REPUTATION HAS SUFFERED!

YOU HAVE A SUGGESTION?
YES, SIR. INSTEAD OF TRYING TO HOLD ON TO OUR FADING IDENTITY AS A COLLEGE, WHY DON'T WE REPOSITION OURSELVES AS A DEMANDING HIGH SCHOOL?
©B Trudeau

DEMANDING?
OKAY, FORGET DEMANDING. THAT COULD BE OFF-PUTTING.

THINK OF IT, SIR. INSTEAD OF BEING A SO-SO COLLEGE, WE COULD BECOME THE FINEST HIGH SCHOOL IN THE COUNTRY!
NO, CAMPBELL, I'M NOT READY TO GIVE UP ON THIS PLACE JUST YET...

I'VE TALKED TO SOME OF THESE KIDS—THEY'RE SMART! THEIR ONLY PROBLEM IS THAT THEIR EDUCATIONS LEFT THEM IGNORANT!

OKAY, HOW ABOUT A **JUNIOR** COLLEGE?
NO, THE ATHLETIC DEPARTMENT WOULD RAISE HELL.
©B Trudeau

HI, FOLKS! CAUGHT YOU READING THE **SUNDAY COMICS**, DIDN'T I?
DON'T BE EMBARRASSED— **MILLIONS** OF FOLKS READ 'EM!

EVER WONDER WHERE ALL THE **IDEAS** COME FROM?
WELL, BELIEVE IT OR NOT, WE'RE OFTEN INSPIRED BY STORIES IN... SHUDDER! THE **REST** OF THE PAPER!

NARRATOR
ONCE THE KERNEL OF AN IDEA HAS BEEN FOUND, CRACK TEAMS OF RESEARCHERS, WRITERS AND ARTISTS DEVELOP A STORY IN **DOZENS** OF DRAFTS AND PREPARATORY SKETCHES!

OF COURSE, NOT ALL IDEAS ARE CREATED EQUAL — NOT BY A LONG SHOT!

EVEN AFTER **WEEKS** OF DEVELOPMENT SOME STRIPS — LIKE THIS ONE — HAVE TO BE **SCRAPPED!**

DISAPPOINTING? YOU BET!
BUT THAT'S WHAT QUALITY CONTROL IS **ALL ABOUT!**
FWIP!
GB Trudeau

YOU WANTED TO SEE ME, SIR?
YES, LLOYD, I WANTED TO TALK TO YOU ABOUT THAT DAMN VIDEO...

WHAT VIDEO IS THAT, SIR?
THE TAPE THAT JERRY FALWELL HAS BEEN PEDDLING ON HIS SHOW WITH PHIL CRANE'S ENDORSEMENT.

I'M AFRAID I HAVEN'T SEEN IT, SIR.
WELL, YOU SHOULD! IT ACCUSES ME OF SEXUAL HARASSMENT, OF COCAINE ADDICTION, OF RUNNING A MONEY-LAUNDERING OPERATION FOR A DRUG RING...

...AND OF ORDERING THE BEATINGS AND MURDERS OF SEVERAL POLITICAL OPPONENTS! CAN YOU BELIEVE IT? FALWELL AND CRANE ARE ACCUSING ME OF **MURDER**!

THAT'S ASTONISHING, SIR. IT'D BE IN-CREDIBLY VILE IF IT WEREN'T SO LUDICROUS!
WELL, EXACTLY. WHAT DO YOU THINK I SHOULD DO?

UM... IGNORE IT?
REALLY? I WAS THINKING OF A COVER-UP.

THE WIDOW DOONESBURY FIRST NOTICED HIM ON THE KNOLL ABOVE THE OLD MANION PLACE...
HMM... WHO IS THAT MAN? AND WHAT'S HE DOING?

HER CURIOSITY GOT THE BETTER OF HER.
GOOD MORNIN', MA'AM!
MORNIN'.

I'M JUST DOING SOME SURVEYING. NOT DISTURBING YOU, AM I?
NO...NO, I SUPPOSE NOT.

THAT NIGHT, SHE GOT THE FRETS.
I BETTER CALL THE PRISON.
MAYBE HE'S ONE OF THEIRS.
GBTrudeau

IN THE DAYS THAT FOLLOWED, THE WIDOW DOONESBURY KEPT A VIGILANT EYE ON THE STRANGER.
HE'S STILL OUT THERE!

WELL, HELLO AGAIN!
HELLO. STILL "SURVEYING"?

YUP. SURE IS NICE OF YOU TO KEEP STOPPING BY, MA'AM.
UM...NOT AT ALL! GOOD DAY!
GBTrudeau

LATER, AT SHERIFF TOWNSEND'S OFFICE...
WHAT KIND OF CRIME SPREE, MRS. D?
HOW SHOULD I KNOW? THAT'S YOUR JOB!

THE WIDOW COULD NO LONGER CONTAIN HER CURIOSITY.
WHAT AM I "UP TO," MA'AM?
YES.

WELL, MA'AM, I'M PART OF A CREATIVE TEAM. WE'RE BUILDING SOMETHING MAGICAL HERE— A SPECIAL PLACE OF DREAMS!
UH-OH...HE'S FROM DISNEY!

I'LL BE EXPLAINING IT ALL AT A TOWN MEETING TONIGHT. WON'T YOU COME?
AND DON'T WORRY—I'M NOT FROM DISNEY.

THAT EVENING...
I STILL SMELL MOUSE.
GBTrudeau

AT THAT NIGHT'S TOWN MEETING, THE STRANGER ROSE TO HIS FEET...
GOOD PEOPLE, MY NAME IS DANNY DOYLE...

AS SOME OF YOU MAY KNOW, I'VE SPENT THE WEEK SURVEYING OUT AT THE MANION PLACE. THE FOLKS I WORK FOR ARE HOPING TO DEVELOP IT INTO SOMETHING QUITE SPECIAL...

WE PROPOSE TO BUILD A FIELD OF DREAMS, ACTUALLY, A WHOLE **WORLD** OF DREAMS! 120,000 SQ. FT. OF **SHOPPERS' PARADISE**!

HOLD IT! I OWN A SMALL FAMILY STORE...
BUT YOUR SELECTION STINKS, ED! LET THE MAN SPEAK!

AT THE TOWN MEETING, RUBY KILGORE WAS SKEPTICAL...
MR. DOYLE, YOU SAY YOU'RE BUILDING A "SHOPPERS' PARADISE"...

WELL, WHAT KIND OF **VALUE** ARE YOU TALKING ABOUT? LIKE, HOW MUCH WOULD A 24-COUNT PACKAGE OF EXTRA-LARGE PAMPERS COST ME?

ONE LOW PRICE—$5.99! YES, $5.99! BUY THREE, YOUR COST IS ONLY **$14.99**!
GASP!

BOY'S TURTLENECKS, FROM **$2.49**! RADIAL TIRES, ONLY **$29.50**!
DON'T **LISTEN** TO HIM! THOSE ARE THE **DEVIL'S** PRICES!
OOH...
AHH...

THE STRANGER COMES CLEAN...
SO WHAT DO WE CALL OUR 120,000 SQ. FT. OF EXCITEMENT?

WELL, WE CALL IT THE PEOPLE'S EMPORIUM, BUT **YOU** KNOW IT BY THE NAME **WAL-MART**!

WAL-MART?

...INSTANTLY DIVIDING THE TOWN.
MY BUSINESS IS **RUINED**!
FINALLY! ONE-STOP SHOPPING!
A WAY OF LIFE—**GONE**!
GOOD RIDDANCE!

THE ASSEMBLED CITIZENRY COULD SCARCELY BELIEVE THEIR EARS...
WAL-MART?
YES, WAL-MART!

NOW, WE KNOW YOUR CONCERNS, BUT BELIEVE ME, THE OUTLET WE ENVISION HERE WILL BE THE **PRIDE** OF THE REGION!

FIRST OF ALL, IN THE DESIGN OF THE STRUCTURE, WE'LL RESPECT THE UNIQUE AGRARIAN CHARACTER OF THE SURROUNDING COUNTRYSIDE – TO THE POINT OF PLANTING **SOYBEANS** ON THE ROOF!

THE DREAM TAKES SHAPE.
MOOO!
WAL-MART
WAL-MART
ENTRANCE

HERB BAUSER, OF HERB'S SUNDRIES, TAKES ON THE MAN FROM WAL-MART...
HOW'S THE LOCAL MERCHANT SUPPOSE TO SURVIVE IN YOUR SHADOW?
TELL HIM, HERB!

YOU'LL **KILL OFF** OUR DOWNTOWN!
THAT'S JUST A MYTH, HERB! ONCE THEY ADJUST, LOCAL BUSINESSES WILL FLOURISH AS **NEVER** BEFORE!

YOU SEE, BECAUSE OF OUR OBVIOUS ADVANTAGES, WE'LL FORCE YOU TO RUN A SHARPER OPERATION – MUCH MORE FOCUSED AND RESPONSIVE TO YOUR CUSTOMERS!

WELL, GOSH! YOU'D DO THAT FOR ME?
HECK, YES! IT'S ALL PART OF OUR TOUGH LOVE PROGRAM FOR LOCAL RETAILERS!

LOCAL PHARMACIST GILBERT WAX HAD HEARD ENOUGH.
IT'S NOT **FAIR!** I'M A THIRD-GENERATION DRUGGIST! YOU'LL **RUIN** ME!

NOW, GIL, YOU HAVE NOTHING TO WORRY ABOUT. WAL-MART WILL SERVE AS A MAGNET, CREATING A BOON FOR **ALL** LOCAL STORES!
OH, RIGHT...

YOUR 20,000 SQ. FT. SUPERPHARMACY IS GOING TO ACT AS A DRAW FOR MY 600 SQ. FT. DRUG STORE? I DON'T THINK SO!

THEN SELL SOMETHING ELSE. LOCAL CRAFTS! CORNCOB PIPES.
CORNCOB PIPES?
I COULD SOURCE THOSE FOR YOU, GIL.

IT WAS GINNY MAYHEW'S TURN.
MR. DOYLE, WE OWN AN APPLIANCE STORE. IF YOU COME IN HERE, WE'RE DEAD MEAT.

WELL, AGAIN, IT MAY BE THAT YOU JUST NEED A CHANGE! YOU COULD CARRY KNICK-KNACKS, FOR INSTANCE.
KNICK-KNACKS?

HEAR THAT, MOM? WE DON'T HAVE TO SELL DISHWASHERS ANYMORE! WE CAN SWITCH TO KNICK-KNACKS!
KNICK-KNACKS! IT'S LIKE A DREAM COME TRUE! IF ONLY YOUR FATHER WERE ALIVE!
©B Trudeau

YOU KNOW, FOR RUSTICS, YOU FOLKS SURE ARE GIVEN TO SARCASM.
SO WE WATCH LETTERMAN. SUE US.

THE MAN FROM WAL-MART TRIED A DIFFERENT TACK...
YOU KNOW, FOLKS, YOU ALL HAVE BEEN FOCUSING ON THE DOWNSIDE OF WAL-MART...

BUT THERE'S A LOT OF GOOD NEWS ABOUT WAL-MART AS WELL! FOR STARTERS, NO MORE LONG TRIPS TO TULSA FOR BASIC NECESSITIES!

THEN THERE'S ECONOMIC DEVELOPMENT! PEOPLE WILL BE COMING INTO THIS AREA TO SPEND MONEY FROM AS FAR AWAY AS DENISON AND WICHITA FALLS!
©B Trudeau

HOLD IT! YOU'RE BRINGING TEXAS TRASH IN HERE?
OH, GOSH! WHAT IS THIS, SOME SORT OF FRIENDLY RIVALRY?

WELL, FOLKS, I WANT TO THANK YOU FOR ALL YOUR FEEDBACK! I'LL BE PRESENTING OUR PROPOSAL TO YOUR PLANNING BOARD SOON...
LOOKS LIKE WE'RE ALL HERE...

UH... REALLY? WELL, I KNOW YOU'LL WANT TO DEBATE THIS! THE TOWN IS CLEARLY DIVIDED!
THINK SO? LET'S VOTE NOW. ALL IN FAVOR, SAY AYE!

WAIT A MINUTE! YOU CAN'T JUST...
ALL OPPOSED, SAY NAY!
NAY!!

THE MAN FROM WAL-MART NEVER KNEW WHAT HIT HIM.
'NIGHT!
'NIGHT!
'NIGHT!
MY GOD...WHAT'LL I TELL MY CORPORATE MASTERS?
©B Trudeau

Exit Wound: Can now prove O.J. was in Dallas. Yrs., Dal-Tex.
Dal-Tex: Good work. Exit Wound.
TAP! TAP!
TAP!

WHEW! DON'T PRO-FESSIONAL CONSPIRACY THEORISTS JUST TAKE YOUR BREATH AWAY?
WHETHER THEY'RE ON ABOUT O.J. OR CLINTON OR J.F.K., TODAY'S GASSY KNOT-HEADS ARE IN FULL CRY!

ONE CONVENIENT FEATURE OF A CONSPIRACY THEORY IS THAT IT CAN NEVER BE DISPROVED. WHY? BECAUSE ANY OFFICIAL INQUIRY IS ALWAYS CON-DUCTED BY PEOPLE IN-VOLVED IN THE CON-SPIRACY!

EXPERTS BELIEVE THAT CONSPIRACY THEORY FLOURISHES DURING TIMES OF PUBLIC MISTRUST AND CYNICISM! BUT THESE "EXPERTS" MAY BE IN THE EMPLOY OF ALIENS! SEE WHAT I MEAN?

WHAT TO DO? DO WHAT I DO—USE A LITTLE COM-MON SENSE! SURE, BE SKEPTICAL, BUT GO WITH THE OCCASION-AL REALITY CHECK!

AFTER ALL, SOME THINGS REALLY ARE WHAT THEY SEEM!
ORP!
©GBTrudeau

YOU KNOW, WE HAVEN'T TALKED SINCE SAUGERTIES, CORNELL! WHAT WAS IT LIKE?
MEGA-TRIPPY, MAN! OUTASIGHT AND THEN SOME!

"THE PARKING LOTS WERE FULL, SO WE HAD TO HIKE IN FROM VERMONT..."

"THE CAMPING SITES WERE SO CROWDED AND UNSANITARY THAT MALARIA BROKE OUT..."

"... BUT THE MOSHING WAS EXCELLENT, AS WAS THE FAST FOOD, THE ECO-VILLAGE AND EVEN THE MUSIC!"

IT JUST DOESN'T GET ANY BETTER THAN WOODSTOCK TWO, MAN! I'M STILL HAVING TROUBLE ACCEPTING THAT IT'S OVER...

BUT YOU HAVE TO, CORNELL. YOU HAVE TO LET GO.
I'M TRYING, MAN.

BOOPSIE! MAKE ME HAPPY I TOOK YOUR CALL!
OKAY! ARE YOU SITTING DOWN?

I'M ALWAYS SITTING DOWN. IT'S A POINT OF HONOR.
WE'VE DECIDED TO BAPTIZE SAM, AND GUESS WHO WE BOOKED!

I DUNNO. THE POPE?
BETTER! ARIANNA-JOHN HUFFINGTON, MINISTER OF LIGHT, IN JOHN-ROGER'S MOVEMENT OF SPIRITUAL INNER AWARENESS...

PLEASE, PLEASE, DON'T INVITE ME!
AND WE WANT YOU TO BE SAM'S GOD-FATHER-JOHN!
©B Trudeau

IT WAS NICE OF YOU TO COME ON SUCH SHORT NOTICE, SID! ISN'T IT A BEAUTIFUL DAY FOR A BAPTISM?
UM... I GUESS SO. WILL THIS TAKE LONG?

I DON'T IMAGINE SO. MINISTER ARIANNA-JOHN HAS A VERY TIGHT SCHEDULE. BUT YOU SHOULD SEE SAM — SHE'S SO EXCITED! ESPECIALLY WHEN SHE HEARD YOU'D BE HER GOD-FATHER-JOHN!

MOMMY? WHAT'S GOING ON?
OH, THERE YOU ARE, SWEETIE! REMEMBER MOMMY'S AGENT, UNCLE SID?
HI, KID.

DADDY SAYS YOU'RE A BLOOD-SUCKING WEASEL.
HE HAS TO BE, HON. IT'S HIS JOB.
IS THERE AN OPEN BAR?
©B Trudeau

MOMMY, WHO'S THAT STRANGE LADY?
THAT'S ARIANNA-JOHN HUFFINGTON, HON!

SHE'S A MINISTER OF LIGHT IN JOHN-ROGER'S MOVEMENT OF SPIRITUAL INNER AWARENESS, AND SHE'S GOING TO BAPTIZE YOU!

DEARLY BELOVED! WHO SEEKS TO ANOINT THIS CHILD INTO THE SOUL REALM OF THE MYSTICAL TRAVELER CONSCIOUSNESS?
WE DO, YOUR INSIGHTFULNESS!

AND THE CHILD'S NAME?
SAMANTHA-ROGER MOONBALL.
HOLD IT.
©B Trudeau

AND NOW IN THE NAME OF JOHN-ROGER, EMBODIMENT OF MYSTICAL TRAVELER CONSCIOUSNESS...
YOU KNOW, THERE'S SOMETHING VERY FAMILIAR ABOUT ARIANNA-JOHN.

I THEE BAPTIZE SAMANTHA-ROGER MOONBALL!
WELL, SHE'S MARRIED TO ROY-MICHAEL HUFFINGTON JR., THE GUY WHO'S RUNNING FOR SENATE!

AIEE! MOMMY! SHE GOT ME ALL WET!
HE'S RIGHT OVER THERE...
HUFFINGTON'S MARRIED TO A CULT MINISTER?

FLY, MY LITTLE MYSTICAL TRAVELER, FLY!
YOU FLY! IT'S MY HOUSE!
IT'S GETTING TOO WEIRD TO BE A CONSERVATIVE.
GB Trudeau

SID, I'D LIKE YOU TO MEET ARIANNA-JOHN'S HUSBAND, ROY-MICHAEL HUFFINGTON JR.
HUFFINGTON?

YOU'RE THE GUY SPENDING $20 MILLION OF FAMILY MONEY TO GET A SENATE SEAT, RIGHT?
WHY, YES! YOU'VE HEARD OF ME!

KIND OF UNAVOIDABLE. YOU MUST REALLY WANT THE JOB IN A BAD WAY, GUY!
WELL, I'VE NEVER REALLY DONE ANYTHING. I'M TRYING TO PROVE MYSELF TO MY FATHER.

HEY, BEEN THERE. BUT THE OLD COOT DIED ON ME.
THEN I'VE GOT YOUR VOTE?
GB Trudeau

SO MICHAEL-ROY! PITCH ME, BABE! WHY YOU IN THE SENATE?
WELL, I HAVEN'T DONE MUCH, SO I GUESS IT'S THE CHARACTER THING.

CHARACTER? HELLO? I READ, BABE! YOUR COMPANY BLEW OFF $7 MILLION IN UNPAID TAXES! AND YOU WERE FINED $250,000 FOR SHIPPING SHOCK BATONS TO FOREIGN DICTATORS!

HEY, THOSE THINGS WERE NOT UNDER MY CONTROL! I WAS TOTALLY OUT OF THE LOOP! IT WASN'T MY RESPONSIBILITY! IT WAS SOMEONE ELSE'S FAULT!

I THINK YOU'RE READY FOR THE SENATE, BABE.
OH... THANKS. WHAT DO YOU MEAN?
GB Trudeau

SID'S STILL SCHMOOZING WITH SENATE WANNABE MICHAEL-ROY HUFFINGTON.
PEOPLE ASK ME WHAT I'VE ACCOMPLISHED IN MY 21 MONTHS IN CONGRESS...

WELL, THE ANSWER IS LOTS! I PLANNED MY SENATE CAMPAIGN, I LINED UP MY ADVERTISING TEAM, I RETURNED PHONE CALLS, I RESTED UP!

INTERESTING. YOU KNOW, MICHAEL-ROY, THE CLOSER I LOOK AT YOU AND YOUR RECORD, I... I...
YES?

NEVER MIND, I'M SURE IT'S JUST ME.
WHAT? WHAT?

BY THE WAY, MICHAEL-ROY, WHAT'S THE DEAL ON THE CRIME BILL? I HEAR YOU VOTED BOTH FOR IT AND AGAINST IT!
TRUE...

THE REASON I DID THAT IS BECAUSE IT TURNED OUT THAT SOME VOTERS WERE FOR IT, AND SOME AGAINST IT!

YOU SEE, SID-JOHN, I'M INTO INCLUSIVENESS! IT'S PART OF MY LIFE-FORCE! I WANT TO BE A SENATOR FOR ALL THE PEOPLE!

UH-HUH. WHO THOUGHT THAT ONE UP—MINISTER GET-A-LIFE?
SHE HELPED WITH THE FINAL WORDING, YES.

SID-JOHN, YOU'RE PROBABLY WONDERING—WHO IS THE REAL MICHAEL-ROY JR.? WELL, HE'S A FELLAH WHO FEELS PASSIONATELY THAT ELECTIVE OFFICES ARE FOR SALE!
M-R

I BELIEVE IN THAT MESSAGE! IN FACT, DURING MY HOUSE CAMPAIGN I SPENT $80 FOR EVERY VOTE I GOT—JUST TO GET THAT MESSAGE OUT!

NOW, THERE WILL BE CYNICS, DOUBTERS WHO SAY A SENATE SEAT CAN'T BE BOUGHT. BUT I'M OUT TO PROVE THAT THEY'RE WRONG, WRONG, WRONG!

GOOD FOR YOU! SAY, COULD I HAVE MY 80 BUCKS UP FRONT?
SURE! WHERE'S MY WALLET BOY! HEY, KID! OVER HERE!

SO WHAT'D YOU THINK OF MICHAEL-ROY, SID? ISN'T HE THE NICEST?

I GUESS. BIT OF AN EMPTY SUIT, THOUGH.
WELL, I THINK THAT'S SO ARI-ANNA-JOHN CAN WEAR IT. THEY SHARE **EVERYTHING!**

WHERE'D YOU MEET HIM, ANYWAY?
ON THE BEACH. HE'D JUST MOVED IN FROM TEXAS SO HE COULD REPRESENT US...
©B'Trudeau

HEY, Y'ALL! WHERE'S THE OCEAN?
UH... TO YOUR LEFT. THE BLUE THING.

REALLY? YOU KNEW MICHAEL-ROY DURING HIS EARLY CALIFORNIA YEARS?
SURE! WE GO ALL THE WAY BACK TO 1992!

"WE HIT IT OFF INSTANTLY..."
SO AFTER I CASHED OUT OF DAD'S COMPANY, I HAD TO DO **SOMETHING!** SO I BOUGHT A HOUSE IN CALIFORNIA!

I DIDN'T ACTUALLY MOVE IN—THE TAX SITUATION WAS TOO PERFECT IN TEXAS—BUT MY WIFE WENT OUT TO ESTABLISH A BEACHHEAD! THEN AT THE LAST MINUTE, I JOINED HER AND BOUGHT A CONGRESSIONAL SEAT!
M-R

WOW! YOU SOUND LIKE A MAN WITH A DREAM!
MORE LIKE A SCHEME. LIKE MY CANDOR? IT'S MY WIFE'S IDEA.
©B'Trudeau

YOU KNOW, MICHAEL-ROY, I FEEL LIKE I KNOW YOU FROM SOME PLACE, PERHAPS FROM ONE OF MY OTHER LIVES.
REALLY?

YES. YOU WEREN'T ALIVE IN 15TH CENTURY PATAGONIA, BY ANY CHANCE, WERE YOU? OR IN SAVANNAH, GEORGIA, DURING THE RECONSTRUCTION?

UM... WELL... THIS IS A LITTLE EMBARRASSING TO ADMIT TO A FELLOW NEW-AGER.
WHAT? WHAT IS IT, MICHAEL-ROY?
©B'Trudeau

WELL, I'M NOT SURE I EVER **HAD** A FORMER LIFE!
GOSH! WELL, ARE YOU HAVING ONE NOW?

BEFORE WE TALK ABOUT THE MID-TERM, A FEW WORDS ABOUT GRADING...

AS MANY OF YOU MAY KNOW, I USED TO VIEW GRADING AS AN OCCASION FOR ACCOUNTABILITY. HOWEVER, A RECENT LAWSUIT HAS COMPELLED ME TO FACTOR IN CONSIDERATIONS UNRELATED TO MERIT.

I'M REFERRING, OF COURSE, TO VICTIMHOOD. IF YOU BELONG TO A VICTIM GROUP, BY VIRTUE OF GENDER, RACE, RELIGION, ETHNICITY, CLASS, FAMILY DYSFUNCTION, DISABILITY OR ADDICTION, PLEASE REGISTER YOUR STATUS WITH THE DEAN BEFORE MID-TERMS ARE GIVEN.

AGAIN, YOU **MUST** BE A FULLY REGISTERED VICTIM TO RECEIVE SPECIAL CONSIDERATION OVER NON-VICTIMS, WHO WILL STILL BE GRADED ON ACTUAL PERFORMANCE!

SINCE MID-TERMS START NOVEMBER 1, THE CUT-OFF FOR REGISTRATION IS OCTOBER 31. ANY QUESTIONS?

YEAH! DOESN'T A CUT-OFF DISCRIMINATE AGAINST THE TIME-IMPAIRED?
NO. EXTENSIONS WILL BE GRANTED TO THE CLUELESS.
©B. Trudeau

ANYONE WANT A SECTION OF THE PAPER?

THE PAPER? YOU STILL READ THE PAPER? HOW COME, CORNELL?
NEWS, BOOPSIE. TO FIND OUT WHAT'S GOING ON.

BUT THAT'S WHAT "ENTERTAINMENT TONIGHT" IS FOR.
WHOA... WE'VE REALLY SLIPPED INTO POST-LITERACY, HAVEN'T WE? NO WONDER NEWSPAPERS ARE IN SUCH TROUBLE...

THE TUBE RULES, TOTALLY. PEOPLE BUY PAPERS FOR THE TV AND MOVIE LISTINGS. THEY BUY MAGAZINES FOR THE PICTURES. THEY STILL BUY ACTUAL BOOKS, BUT THEY RARELY FINISH READING THEM.

WOW... THAT'S PRETTY SCARY...

WILL ANYONE FINISH READING **THIS?**
GOOD QUESTION.
BOYS! GIRLS! DID **YOU** MAKE IT THIS FAR? YOU **MAY** HAVE WON A VALUABLE PRIZE!
CHECK WITH THIS NEWSPAPER!
GBTrudeau

HI, KIDS! WELCOME TO THE KICK-OFF OF NATIONAL "CHARACTER COUNTS" WEEK! ALL THIS WEEK, WE–AND MANY OTHERS–WILL BE DISCUSSING CHARACTER!

BY PRESIDENTIAL PROCLAMATION, THIS WEEK HAS BEEN DESIGNATED A TIME TO CELEBRATE AND PROMOTE SHARED VALUES ESSENTIAL TO GOOD CHARACTER!

OVER 30 STATES HAVE SIGNED ON TO PROMOTE THE "SIX PILLARS OF CHARACTER": RESPONSIBILITY, TRUSTWORTHINESS, RESPECT, CARING, FAIRNESS AND CITIZENSHIP!
UM... WHAT ABOUT THE OTHER 20 STATES?
BUSINESS AS USUAL! PARTY ON, YOU GUYS!

HI, KIDS! WELCOME TO DAY TWO OF NATIONAL "CHARACTER COUNTS" WEEK!

ALL WEEK, WE'LL BE DISCUSSING THE SIX PILLARS OF CHARACTER: TRUSTWORTHINESS, RESPECT, RESPONSIBILITY, FAIRNESS, CARING AND CITIZENSHIP...

FIRST UP, TRUSTWORTHINESS! HERE TO DISCUSS THIS IMPORTANT CORE ELEMENT OF CHARACTER IS OUR OLD FRIEND, ZONKER HARRIS! ZONKER?

UH... ZONKER? ZONKER!
WHAT? I'M IN THE SHOWER!

WELCOME BACK TO DAY THREE OF NATIONAL "CHARACTER COUNTS" DAY! TODAY'S PILLAR IS RESPONSIBILITY–AS EXPLAINED BY OUR GOOD FRIEND MARK!

THANKS, MIKE. I'M HAPPY TO TRY TO EXPLAIN THE IDEA OF RESPONSIBILITY, BUT WHAT IF I CAN'T? WHAT IF I CAN'T COME UP WITH A MEANINGFUL, WORKING DEFINITION?

WELL, TOO BAD! I HAVE A RESPONSIBILITY TO TRY! I'VE MADE A COMMITMENT AND I HAVE TO HONOR IT!
AND YET, ODDLY, YOU HAVEN'T.
WELL, WE'VE RUN OUT OF SPACE! IT'S NOT MY FAULT!

RESPECT: A KEY ELEMENT IN CHARACTER THAT GOVERNS HOW WE TREAT OTHER PEOPLE, RIGHT, B.D.?
UH... RIGHT.

RESPECT, OF COURSE, IS SOMETHING THAT'S EARNED. LET'S LOOK AT AN INSTRUCTIVE EPISODE FROM B.D.'S PAST...
ROLL IT!

HEY, WE WERE DOWN BY TEN, BUT WE CAME BACK AND KICKED BUTT! WE SHOWED CHARACTER! WE FORCED THEM TO RESPECT US!

BUT CAN YOU FORCE SOMEONE TO RESPECT YOU? DOES KICKING BUTT REALLY SHOW CHARACTER?
DAMN BETCHA! LET'S SEE IT AGAIN!
©B Trudeau

PILLAR FOUR: CARING. THIS IS WHERE IT ALL COMES TOGETHER. CARING IS WHAT HOLDS FAMILIES AND COMMUNITIES TOGETHER.

HELLO?
HI, MOM. IT'S ME, DUKE.
YES, EVEN THE MOST HARD-BOILED AMONGST US VALUES CARING!

I KNOW I HAVEN'T CALLED YOU IN A FEW YEARS, BUT I JUST WANTED YOU AND DAD TO KNOW THAT YOU WERE IN MY THOUGHTS.
©B Trudeau

WHO IS THIS, REALLY?
SHE'S BLOWING ME OFF.
IT'S OKAY. YOU SHOWED YOU CARED.

UH-OH! CHARACTER WEEK IS ALMOST OVER, AND WE STILL HAVE TWO PILLARS TO GO! GUESS WE'LL HAVE TO SKIP FAIRNESS!
HEY, WHO SAID LIFE IS FAIR?

THAT JUST LEAVES CITIZENSHIP, THAT MORAL QUALITY SO ESSENTIAL TO THE FUNCTIONING OF ANY SUCCESSFUL COMMUNITY AND NATION...

WHAT'S CITIZENSHIP? IT'S DOING YOUR SHARE, GETTING INVOLVED, VOLUNTEERING SERVICE, CONSERVING RESOURCES—ALL THE TRADITIONAL VALUES OF THE DEMOCRATIC PARTY!
©B Trudeau

ALTHOUGH IN FAIRNESS, THE G.O.P. ALSO EMBRACES THOSE VALUES!
YOU DID IT! YOU GOT FAIRNESS IN!

HELLO?
NAME?

JIMMY THUD-PUCKER!
OKAY, JIMMY, GRAB SOME CANS. LEAD SHEET IS IN FRONT OF YOU.

READY? HERE WE GO! DUET SEVEN, TAKE ONE!

OOH, YEAH... ♫ ♪ YES, SHE **DOES**!... YOU KNOW, IT'S TRUE... **OOH**... ♫ BRING IT ON **HOME**!
OKAY, THAT'S GOT IT!

I'M DONE?
YUP. THANKS FOR COMING IN.

PLEASE TELL MR. SINATRA IT WAS AN HONOR WORKING WITH HIM!
YEAH, FOR HIM, TOO. **NEXT**!

MEANWHILE, BACK IN OLLIE NORTH'S SITUATION ROOM...
CONTROL! IS THE MESS AREA SECURE?
AFFIRMATIVE, COLONEL!

GOOD. I WANT TO GRAB AN M.R.E. BEFORE TONIGHT'S SPEECH. I'M GETTING SICK OF BANQUET RATIONS!
WHO ARE YOU SPEAKING TO, SIR?

TRUE BELIEVERS. IT'S A NO-BRAINER. ALL I HAVE TO DO IS WRAP MYSELF UP IN THE FLAG.
ANY-THING I CAN DO, SIR?

YEAH, I'LL NEED A FRESH ONE. THIS HAS GOT GRAVY STAINS ON IT.
WARDROBE! SEND UP A NEW STARS 'N' BARS! ON THE DOUBLE!

DUKE IS STILL DUTY OFFICER IN OLLIE'S SITUATION ROOM.
MY FRIENDS, WHAT THIS ELECTION COMES DOWN TO IS CHARACTER!

WHO DO YOU WANT REPRE-SENTING YOU— A RECOVER-ING PARTY ANIMAL OR A MAN WHO HAS BEEN...
...CON-VICTED OF FOUR FELONIES?

WHO TRADED ARMS WITH TERRORISTS? WHO SHREDDED EVIDENCE? WHO LIED TO CON-GRESS? WHO STOLE FUNDS?

INCOMING! SECOND BALCONY! TAKE HIM DOWN!
ROGER, CONTROL! WE GOT HIM!
AIEE!

AND I'VE GOT A MESSAGE FOR THE CRIMINAL ELEMENT IN THE GREAT COM-MONWEALTH OF VIR-GINIA: GET OUT! FIND ANOTHER STATE, LIKE NEW YORK!

THE PEOPLE OF VIRGINIA ARE TIRED OF REVOLVING-DOOR JUSTICE, TIRED OF SPINELESS JUDGES...
UH-OH...

...AND TIRED OF HAVING THE CONVICTIONS OF FELONS OVERTURNED ON LEGAL TECHNI-CALITIES!
HEADS UP, COLONEL. YOU JUST DESCRIBED YOURSELF.

I DIDN'T SAY WHAT I JUST SAID! ANYONE WHO SAYS I DID IS A LIAR!
NICE RE-COVERY. BRING IT HOME.

GOOD WORK WITH THAT HECKLER TONIGHT, DUKE...
THANKS, COLONEL.

YOUR TEAM IS GETTING PRETTY DARN EFFICIENT.
THEY'RE MOTIVATED, SIR! THEY'RE TASKED WITH PROTECTING FIRST AMENDMENT RIGHTS!

HEE, HEE! I ALMOST FEEL SORRY FOR THE LEFTIST SCUMBALL...
HOW'S THAT, COLONEL?

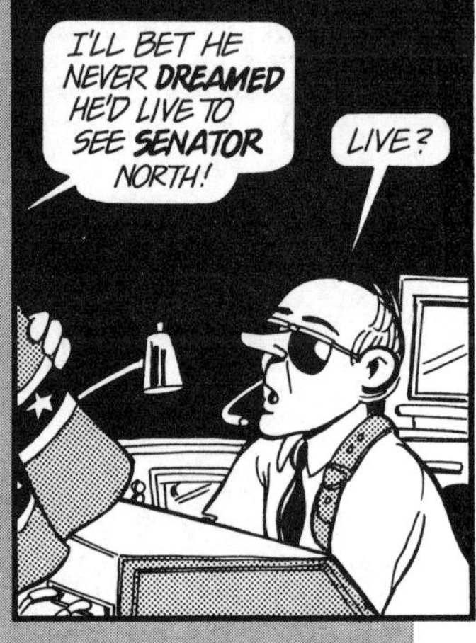
I'LL BET HE NEVER **DREAMED** HE'D LIVE TO SEE **SENATOR** NORTH!
LIVE?

MORE OF THE SAME! THE MEDIA ARE **OBSESSED** WITH MY "LIES"!
I WOULDN'T WORRY ABOUT IT, SIR...

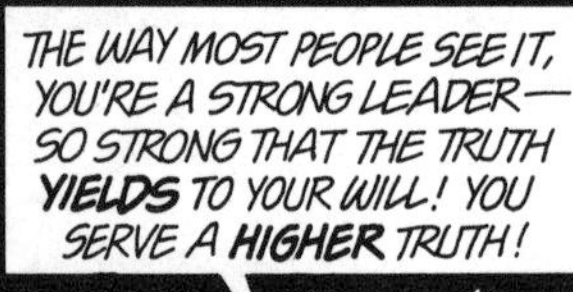
THE WAY MOST PEOPLE SEE IT, YOU'RE A STRONG LEADER—SO STRONG THAT THE TRUTH **YIELDS** TO YOUR WILL! YOU SERVE A **HIGHER** TRUTH!

THE ONLY PROBLEM IS DATA FLOW. WHEN YOU TELL ONE LIE, AND THEN YOU HAVE TO TELL ANOTHER, AND THEN ANOTHER... WHAT'S THAT CALLED?

MISSION CREEP.
RIGHT. IT'S HARD TO KEEP TRACK OF. THAT'S MY ONLY BEEF.

SO YOU AGREE THAT PEOPLE ARE READY FOR LEADERSHIP THAT DOES WHATEVER IT TAKES?
PERMISSION TO SPEAK FREELY, SIR?

GO.
1996 IS ALMOST HERE! TWO MORE YEARS OF THE WAFFLE, AND PEOPLE WILL BE **SCREAMING** FOR A STRONG COMMANDER IN CHIEF AND HIS LOYAL RIGHT-HAND MAN!

WHO **ARE** YOU, DUKE? DO YOU HAVE A RESUMÉ?
I THOUGHT YOU'D NEVER ASK.

YEAH, THIS IS MOBILE SECURITY. GIVE ME THE COL-ONEL!
THIS IS NORTH!
COL-ONEL? SMALL CRISIS...

THERE'S A REPORT JUST OUT ABOUT FBI FILES FOUND IN YOUR WHITE HOUSE SAFE. THEY DESCRIBE ALLEGATIONS THAT KEY MEMBERS OF YOUR CONTRA ARMS RESUPPLY TEAM WERE COCAINE TRAFFICKERS!

UH-HUH. AND WHERE DID YOU SEE THAT COCK-AND-BULL STORY?
©B Trudeau

UM... IN THE COMICS.
GET A GRIP, OKAY?

BREAK IT DOWN FOR ME, DUKE.
WELL, COLONEL, BA-SICALLY THE FILES FROM YOUR SAFE SHOW YOU KNEW SOME OF YOUR PEO-PLE WERE SUSPECTED DRUG TRAFFICKERS.

ASSUMING I READ MY OWN FILES. OR THAT THEY WEREN'T PLANTED BY MY ENEMIES. EITHER WAY, LET ME TELL YOU WHERE I COME OUT ON THIS...

IF A MAN'S A TRUE PATRIOT, WILLING TO DO WHAT IT TAKES IN DE-FENSE OF FREEDOM, WHAT HE DOES ON THE SIDE IS HIS BUSINESS! ARE YOU WITH ME HERE?

COLONEL, YOU HAVE NO IDEA.
GOOD. SCRAMBLE THE DIS-INFORMATION TEAM.
©B Trudeau

COLONEL, HOW DO YOU WANT TO HANDLE DAMAGE CONTROL?
FULL COUNTER-STRIKE! IGNORE THE ISSUE AND HIT THE PRESS FOR RAISING IT!

PEOPLE HAVE BEEN AC-CUSING ME OF KNOW-ING WHAT MY OWN PEO-PLE WERE UP TO FOR YEARS! IT WON'T STICK! WHO DO THEY LIST AS SUSPECTED TRAFFICKERS?
CLIKKITY CLIKKITY!

WELL, LET'S SEE... THERE'S... HEY! I KNOW ALL THESE GUYS!
YOU DO?
©B Trudeau

UM... JUST SOCIALLY. FRANKLY, I'M SHOCKED.
ME, TOO. I THOUGHT THEY ONLY SMUGGLED GUNS.

HEADS UP, PEOPLE. THE COLONEL'S TAKING IT TO THE MEDIA!

...AND TODAY, IN AN IMPROMPTU PRESS CONFERENCE AT A GUN FACTORY, MR. NORTH DENIED HE HAD KNOWN THAT SOME OF HIS OPERATIVES WERE SUSPECTED DRUG TRAFFICKERS...

NORTH CONDEMNED ALLEGATIONS THAT FILES FOUND IN HIS SAFE BY THE FBI SHOWED OTHERWISE, SAYING THAT HE HAD NEVER FOUND TIME TO EXAMINE THEM...

THEY WERE IN MY IN-BASKET!
YOUR SAFE HAD AN IN-BASKET?

TO THE PEOPLE OF VIRGINIA, IRAN-CONTRA IS **OLD NEWS!** THIS LATEST "REVELATION" IS JUST MORE FLAK FROM THE **ELITE LIBERAL MEDIA!**

COLONEL, IF THERE'S A LIBERAL BIAS IN THE MEDIA, THEN WHY HAS BILL CLINTON RECEIVED **FAR** WORSE PRESS THAN HIS TWO REPUBLICAN PREDECESSORS?

WELL... UH...

UM...
WE'RE **WAAAITING!**

VOTERS! GRAND OLD PARTY HERE, AND HAVE WE GOT A DEAL FOR YOU!

IT'S CALLED "CONTRACT WITH AMERICA," AND IT HAS SOME VERY ATTRACTIVE FEATURES LIKE TAX CUTS! LOTS OF 'EM! LIKE IT SO FAR?

ADD TO THAT A BALANCED BUDGET AMENDMENT, INCREASED MILITARY SPENDING, AND PAINLESS CUTS IN DOMESTIC SPENDING TO BE DETERMINED LATER, AND WE'VE GOT A BIG WINNER ON OUR HANDS!

WE'RE TALKING BUDGET SURPLUSES! TRICKLE-DOWN EFFECTS! RISING TIDES TO RAISE ALL YACHTS!
J.J., CORRECT ME IF I'M WRONG...

...BUT DIDN'T THE COUNTRY ALREADY FALL FOR THIS ONCE BEFORE?
I BELIEVE THAT MIGHT HAVE BEEN $3 TRILLION IN DEBT AGO.

T-T-TRUST US, US! WE'LL GET IT RIGHT THIS TIME!
I KNEW IT. RERUN.
NUKE HIM.
©B. Trudeau

AH, THOSE AMAZING BUSH BOYS...
NOW, THERE'S A DYNASTY!

NEIL GETS NAILED IN THE S&L SCANDAL, JUNIOR IS ACCUSED OF INSIDER TRADING, AND JEB LOBBIES ON BEHALF OF A BUSINESS ASSOCIATE LATER INDICTED FOR BRIBERY.

WERE THESE KIDS RAISED RIGHT OR WHAT?
GB Trudeau

HEY, NONE OF THEM IN JAIL YET. JUST MARVELOUS. GOTTA BE PROUD.

AFTER MY HUSBAND WAS BRUTALLY KILLED, HIS MURDERER WAS SENTENCED TO DIE...

SURE, GOV. CHILES SIGNED HIS DEATH WARRANT, BUT IF JEB BUSH HAD BEEN IN CHARGE, HE WOULD HAVE EXECUTED HIM ON THE SPOT, PROBABLY USING HIS BARE HANDS!

JEB BUSH, HE'S REALLY, REALLY, REALLY TOUGH ON CRIME!
SOB!
GB Trudeau

JUST MARVELOUS! TAKES ME BACK! WILLIE HORTON CITY!

THE MORNING AFTER, SOMETHING FOR EVERYONE.
YES!
WHEW!

AA·RGGH!

NOOO.
HOORAY!

I LIKE THIS OUTCOME!
NO, I DON'T!
YES, I DO!
NO, I DON'T!
GB Trudeau

WELL, KIDS, I'M OFF TO **VOTE!**
CHIP

COME AGAIN?
I KNOW — IN THE PAST, I'VE MESSED UP. BUT THIS TIME I'VE GOT IT TOGETHER! I'M READY TO EXERCISE MY CONSTITUTIONAL **RIGHT!**

UM... WHY DON'T I DO IT FOR YOU, Z? I'M GOING INTO TOWN ANYWAY.
COULD YOU? I'M RUNNING LATE.
©B Trudeau

ZONK, I GOTTA GO INTO TOWN. I'LL BE BACK IN AN HOUR.
OKAY. DON'T FORGET TO CAST MY VOTE.

OH, RIGHT. WHO DO YOU WANT TO VOTE FOR?
HMM... LET ME SEE...

I'VE BEEN PRETTY UNDECIDED, BUT I GUESS I'LL HAVE TO GO WITH KENNEDY, DOLE, SONNY BONO AND ACE OF BASE!
©B Trudeau

ACE OF BASE?
FOR BEST NEW BAND. OH, WAIT, THEY'RE NOT AMERICAN...

HOW'D IT GO AT THE POLLS, BOOPSIE?
UM... GREAT, ZONK. YOUR VOTE WAS MUCH APPRECIATED.

COOL! WHAT WAS THE MOOD OF OUR FELLOW VOTERS?
IT WAS WEIRD. APPARENTLY WE PREFERRED CANDIDATES WHO WERE UNQUALIFIED.

IN FACT, BEING QUALIFIED SORT OF DISQUALIFIED YOU. KIND OF A FORREST GUMP THING — THE MORE CLUELESS, THE BETTER!
©B Trudeau

YOU'RE **KIDDING!** WHY WASN'T **I** APPROACHED?
WELL, WE ALREADY HAD HUFFINGTON.

HI, FOLKS — MIKE DOONESBURY HERE!

AS YOU MAY KNOW, THERE IS A GROWING DEBATE OVER THE NATURE OF ECONOMIC OPPORTUNITY IN AMERICA.

IN AN INFORMATION-DRIVEN ECONOMY, SOCIETY'S CLASS LINES SEEM INCREASINGLY DETERMINED BY KNOWLEDGE AND INTELLECTUAL MERIT!

MORE THAN AT ANY TIME IN OUR HISTORY, BRAINS, NOT BRAWN, ARE KEY TO ECONOMIC SUCCESS.
WOW... GOOD THING I'M A COLLEGE GRADUATE!

WILL **YOU** BE PART OF THE NEW COGNITIVE ELITE, YOU MAY BE WONDERING? WILL **YOU** MAKE THE CUT?
WHOA... I KNOW **I'M** CURIOUS.

TO FIND OUT, CONTACT ME AT: 72662.3023@compuserve.com.
HOLD IT! WHAT ABOUT THOSE OF US WHO DON'T KNOW HOW TO USE A...
UH-OH.
GBTrudeau

BOOPSIE? WHERE'VE YOU BEEN ALL DAY? IT'S MY DAY OFF!
I TOLD YOU, B.D.—I HAVE JURY DUTY THIS WEEK...

OH, RIGHT... DID YOU GET PICKED?
AS A MATTER OF FACT, I DID. AS AN ALTERNATE.

ALTERNATE. GREAT. I SAW A LOT OF "ALTERNATE" DUTY WHEN I PLAYED FOOT-BALL.
FUNNY YOU SHOULD MENTION FOOT-BALL.

WHAT... NO!
YOU CAN'T TELL A SOUL.
HELLO? IS THIS THE BOOPSTEIN RESIDENCE?
©B Trudeau

WHAT? YOU'RE AN O.J. JUROR?
I'M JUST AN AL-TERNATE, B.D.—AND KEEP IT DOWN.
MOBILE TWO, I'M ON THE PORCH!

BOOPSIE, EVEN AN ALTERNATE CAN CHANGE THE COURSE OF HISTORY!
EXCUSE ME, ARE YOU THE HUSBAND?

OF COURSE, YOU COULD ALSO START A MAJOR RIOT. EITHER WAY, OUR LIVES WILL NEV-ER BE THE SAME!
HELLO?

WHAT?
COULD YOU MOVE YOUR CAR? WE NEED TO SET UP ON YOUR LAWN.
©B Trudeau

MS. BOOP-STEIN! HOW'S IT FEEL TO...
OUT! OUT, YOU PARA-SITES!

MAN! HOW'D THE MEDIA FIND OUT YOU WERE AN O.J. ALTERNATE SO QUICKLY?
BEATS ME. THE ONLY PERSON I TOLD WAS LOIS.

LOIS? LOIS, YOUR PUBLICIST?
SHE'S USUALLY SO DIS-CREET.
©B Trudeau

SURE, WHEN SHE'S PROMOT-ING YOUR FILMS.
B.D., I'M SURE THEY'LL LOSE INTER-EST...
MOBILE ONE, I'M IN! GET ME A FEED!

I COULDN'T BELIEVE I WAS CHOSEN, B.D.! I MEAN, EVERYONE WAS BEING **SO** PARTICULAR!

I THINK I GOT THE GIG WHEN I TOLD THEM I HADN'T READ A NEWSPAPER IN YEARS. THEY ALL JUST SEEMED TO LIGHT UP.

BEFORE I KNEW IT, I WAS ALTERNATES SIX AND SEVEN!
SIX AND SEVEN? BOOPSIE, YOU CAN'T BE TWO ALTERNATES AT THE SAME TIME.
©B Trudeau

SWINE! YOU DARE **CHALLENGE** ME?
WONDERFUL. LIKE THE TRIAL'S NOT A TOTAL ZOO ALREADY.

B.D., WHAT'S GOTTEN INTO YOU?

NOTHING. WHAT DO YOU MEAN?
YOU'VE BEEN STARING AT ME WITH THAT GOOFY GRIN EVER SINCE I GOT HOME!

I DUNNO... IT'S JUST... WELL...
WHAT?
©B Trudeau

I GUESS I JUST CAN'T BELIEVE I'M MARRIED TO AN O.J. ALTERNATE!
WANT ME TO PINCH YOU?

THE CALIFORNIA GOLD RUSH OF '94.
LET'S CUT TO THE CHASE — HOW MUCH FOR EXCLUSIVE RIGHTS TO ALTERNATE SIX'S STORY?

SALLY! GOT THREE HOT ESQUIRES FOR YOUR SHOW! THEY ALL GIVE **KILLER** PRE-TRIAL TALKING HEAD!

THIS IS ROLAND HEDLEY, GROUP LEADER FOR ABC NEWS' **TEAM O.J.!**
©B Trudeau

AS SOON AS I GET A BOOK CONTRACT, I'LL SEND FOR YOU AND THE CHILD.
GOOD LUCK, PA!

AT O.J. CITY...

...THE SPRAWLING MEDIA COMPOUND OUTSIDE THE L.A. COUNTY COURTHOUSE...
K-WAC

...A LONE JOURNALIST ARRIVES...

...TO SEEK HIS FORTUNE.
KNOW WHERE A MAN COULD FIND A BED?
YOUR BEST BET IS GETTING ARRESTED.

RICK, NEWLY ARRIVED IN O.J. CITY, IS SOON BESET BY THE VOICES OF COMMERCE.
YO, BUDDY! SHIRTS HERE!
OJ '94
Free the Juice
PSST! MISTER!

MISTER! YOU WANT TO BUY NICOLE'S TRAINER'S DIARY? ONLY $25!
$25?...

GEE, THAT SOUNDS FAIR...
NO! DON'T DO IT, RICK! IT'S A SCAM! OFF WITH YOU, KID!

WHEW! THANKS, ROLAND.
NO PROBLEM. I DIDN'T WANT YOU TO MAKE THE SAME MISTAKE I DID.

ROLAND! NICE TO SEE A FAMILIAR FACE!
WELCOME TO O.J. CITY, GUY! WHERE YOU STAYING?

WELL, ACTUALLY, I HADN'T WORKED THAT OUT YET...
WELL, THEN YOU BETTER BUNK WITH ME IN MY MAKE-UP TRAILER...

EVERYONE BUNKS ON-SITE?
DAMN BETCHA! THIS IS A VERY COMPETITIVE STORY, GUY! YOU SAY ANYTHING IN YOUR SLEEP, I'LL BREAK IT LIVE BEFORE YOU AWAKE!

THANKS FOR THE WARNING.
I'VE ALREADY GOTTEN THREE SCOOPS THAT WAY...

MAN! LOOK AT ALL THE TRANS-MISSION TRUCKS!
WE CALL THAT AREA NICOLE-VILLE...

IT'S SORT OF A SUBURB OF O.J. CITY — A PRIVILEGED ENCLAVE OF AIR CONDITION-ING AND CATERED BUFFETS...

HERE, WE'VE GOT ALL THE PROBLEMS OF ANY CITY — NOISE, POLLUTION, POOR SANITATION — EVEN BEGGARS!

BEG-GARS!
FOREIGN JOURNAL-ISTS — ALL STARVED FOR LEADS.
HERR AN-CHOR! HERR AN-CHOR!

O.J. CITY IS FULL OF ROUGH MEN, RICK — AND ROUGHER WO-MEN! BEST TO KEEP YOUR WITS ABOUT YOU!
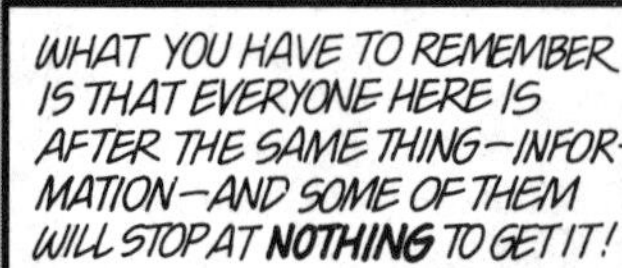
WHAT YOU HAVE TO REMEMBER IS THAT EVERYONE HERE IS AFTER THE SAME THING — INFOR-MATION — AND SOME OF THEM WILL STOP AT **NOTHING** TO GET IT!

THESE PEOPLE ARE UNDER A LOT OF PRESSURE! THEY WORK HARD AND THEY PLAY HAR... HEY, LOOK!
A **COCK FIGHT!**

MY GOD... I DON'T BELIEVE IT...
ME, NEITHER! JUDGE ITO SPECIFICALLY BANNED THEM!

MOMMY, WHEN'S DADDY COMING HOME?
NOT FOR A WHILE, HONEY. THE O.J. TRIAL COULD TAKE MONTHS.

WHERE'S HE STAYING?
AT A BIG MEDIA ENCAMPMENT CALLED O.J. CITY...

I GATHER THE CONDI-TIONS THERE ARE A LITTLE PRIMITIVE. I JUST HOPE YOUR FATHER IS TAKING CARE OF HIMSELF.

20 **BUCKS?** FOR A **POTATO?**
THE ONLY THING CHEAP HERE IS LIFE, RICK.

THE SUNDAY PAPER... STILL A SUBLIME EXPERIENCE!
YUP.

AFTER A LONG WEEK OF INTERFACING WITH ELECTRONIC MEDIA, THERE'S SOMETHING REASSURING ABOUT REAL PAPER BENEATH YOUR FINGERTIPS...

THE EASE OF ACCESS, THE IN-DEPTH ANALYSIS, THE SHARP GRAPHICS AND PHOTOGRAPHY...

AS FAR AS I'M CONCERNED, IT DOESN'T GET ANY BETTER THAN...
WHUMP!
WHAT'S THAT?

OH, MY GO...
AIEE!
WHOA... YOU BOYS OKAY?
I TOLD YOU WE WEREN'T READY FOR DIGITAL!
ZONKER! CALL SUPPORT!
©B Trudeau

HI, DADDY! DID YOU HAVE A NICE DAY?
HI, SWEETHEART. YES, I DID!

WHATCHA DO?
UM ... WELL, ALL SORTS OF THINGS ...

FIRST, I LOOKED OVER MY SCHEDULE. THEN I CHECKED MY E-MAIL AND VOICE MAIL TO SEE IF I HAD ANY IMPORTANT MESSAGES!

AFTER THAT I WATCHED A COUPLE HOURS OF C-SPAN, AND THEN I DOWNLOADED SOME SOFTWARE FROM THE NET, AND THEN, FINALLY, I UNTANGLED THE PHONE CORD.

WOW...

DADDY, WHEN I GROW UP, I WANT TO BE A CONSULTANT, TOO!
WELL, IT'S NOT ALWAYS THAT GLAMOROUS, SWEETHEART.

OKAY, WE'RE STILL TALKING ABOUT SPEAKER-IN-WAITING **NEWT GINGRICH!** IS THE CALLER THERE?
YES, I AM!

MARK, GINGRICH SAYS THE LIBERAL MEDIA ELITE HATE HIM BECAUSE HE'S CONSERVATIVE. MYTH OR REALITY?
TOTAL MYTH...

THE MEDIA DON'T LOATHE NEWT BECAUSE HE'S CONSERVATIVE—WE LOATHE HIM BECAUSE HE'S **GENUINELY** LOATHSOME!
GB Trudeau

OH... SO IT'S PERSONAL.
RIGHT. ACTUALLY, WE'RE STARTING TO **WARM** TO CONSERVATIVES!

MARK, I HEAR THE NEWTMEISTER SLID INTO CONGRESS USING THE WORST SMEAR TACTICS SINCE NIXON IN '46! TRUE?

ABSOLUTELY! AND THAT'S BEEN THE HALLMARK OF HIS PUBLIC LIFE EVER SINCE! A RECKLESS DISREGARD FOR TRUTH, THE DEFAMING OF OPPONENTS AS TRAITORS...

AS FOR HIS PRIVATE LIFE, WELL, DON'T ASK!
I WOULDN'T, EXCEPT HE'S MADE IT GERMANE. DISH ON!
GB Trudeau

THINK BILL CLINTON—ONLY WITHOUT STATE TROOPERS.
WOW... SO HE REALLY **DOES** PUT TAXPAYERS FIRST!
NPR

GETTING TO KNOW **NEWT**...
MARK, I UNDERSTAND MR. FAMILY VALUES HAD A PRETTY MESSY DIVORCE...
YOU MIGHT SAY THAT...

IT HAPPENED WHEN HIS WIFE WAS STRUGGLING WITH CANCER. RIGHT AFTER HER OPERATION, GINGRICH SHOWED UP IN HER HOSPITAL ROOM AND PRESENTED HER WITH A DIVORCE SETTLEMENT!

BUT THAT'S... THAT'S **APPALLING!** I CAN'T EVEN **IMAGINE** SUCH A SCENE!

IMAGINING SUCH A SCENE.
NEWT, I'M... I'M TOO GROGGY TO...
DAMMIT, WOMAN! STOP WHINING AND SIGN!
GB Trudeau

NEWT PICKS HIS MOMENT.
DIVORCE? BUT I... I HAVE CANCER...
PRESS HARD. YOU'RE MAKING TWO COPIES.

FROM THERE, CALLER, IT WAS ALL DOWNHILL! NEWT FIGURED THAT $100 A WEEK SHOULD BE SUFFICIENT SUPPORT FOR HIS FORMER FAMILY...

HIS SICK WIFE AND TWO DAUGHTERS BECAME SO DESTITUTE, THEIR PASTOR HAD TO ASK THEIR FELLOW CHURCH MEMBERS FOR ASSISTANCE.
MAN! I CAN'T IMAGINE A SCENE THAT PITIFUL!

IMAGINING A SCENE THAT PITIFUL.
LET US NOW PRAY FOR THE GINGRICH CHILDREN...
I SHOULDA JUST PUT 'EM IN AN ORPHANAGE!
FOOD DONAT

SO WHAT DOES THE NEWT-MAN HAVE TO SAY ABOUT THE DISPARITY BETWEEN HIS PROFESSED VALUES AND HIS OWN BEHAVIOR?

WHEN I ASKED HIM IN AN EXCLUSIVE INTERVIEW OUTSIDE HIS OFFICE, THIS WAS HIS RESPONSE...
GET THE HELL OUT OF MY FACE!

LATER, WHEN I CALLED TO ASK HIM ABOUT THE ETHICS COMMITTEE INVESTIGATION OF HIS POLITICAL ACTION COMMITTEE, HE HAD THIS TO SAY...
CLIK!

AND HERE'S NEWT ON WHY HE WON'T DISCLOSE THE NAMES OF HIS PAC'S DONORS...
PERVERT! HIPPIE! TRAITOR! CLIK!

OKAY, WE'VE GOT TIME FOR JUST ONE MORE. IS THE CALLER THERE?
YES, I AM, MARK...

I JUST WANTED TO THANK YOU FOR AN ABSOLUTELY SPLENDID EVENING OF PUBLIC AFFAIRS PROGRAMMING!

BEFORE YOUR SHOW, I WOULD HAVE SAID THAT GINGRICH IS JUST A RIGHT-WING NUT. NOW I KNOW HE'S A MEAN, VICIOUS, HYPOCRITICAL RIGHT-WING NUT! HATS OFF TO YOU AND NPR!

WELL, THANKS, MAN! WE DO TRY TO BE EDUCATIONAL...
DO YOU FOLKS ACCEPT DONATIONS? YOU SHOULD!

WHAT? WHAT IS IT, MIKE?
IT'S BUTTS AGAIN...

HE'S BACK ON THE HILL, ONLY THIS TIME THE G.O.P.'S RUNNING THE COMMITTEES!

WOW... TALK ABOUT YOUR NIGHTMARE SCENARIO...

SIR, THIS COMMITTEE OWES YOU A FULL APOLOGY!
EXCELLENT! I ACCEPT!

MIKE'S NIGHTMARE SCENARIO.
MR. BUTTS, FOR THE FIRST TIME IN YEARS, YOU HAVE FRIENDS ON THIS COMMITTEE!
YEA!

...AND WE'LL GET STARTED AS SOON AS THE NEW CHAIRMAN ARRIVES!
OH... THE CHAIRMAN!

I ALMOST FORGOT— THE CHAIRMAN'S SQUARELY IN MY POCKET!

HE'S WHERE?
♪ OH, MR. CHAIRMAN!
TIME TO BOOO-GIE!
BE RIGHT OUT!

MR. BUTTS?
ENJOY THE AUTOGRAPH, SENATOR!

MR. BUTTS? IF WE COULD START?
YO! I'M ALL EARS!
PIZZA

MR. BUTTS, I HOPE YOU REALIZE THAT EVEN THOUGH YOU ARE NOW AMONG ALLIES, WE STILL MIGHT HAVE TO ASK THE OCCASIONAL TOUGH QUESTION.
I UNDERSTAND, CONGRESSMAN.

NOW, THEN, SIR! WHICH IS MORE SATISFYING, MENTHOL OR REGULAR?
YIKES! THAT IS A TOUGH ONE! LET ME THINK...
PIZZA

MR. BUTTS, THE AMERICAN PEOPLE OWE YOU AN APOLOGY...
REALLY?

FOR **YEARS**, THEIR REPRESENTATIVES ON THIS COMMITTEE HAVE RUTHLESSLY HOUNDED YOUR INDUSTRY...
TRUE!

...INVESTIGATING YOU, DEMONIZING YOU, TAXING YOU! WELL, SIR, YOUR NIGHTMARE IS OVER! **FREEDOM** IS BACK IN TOWN!
KOOL!
©B Trudeau

LET THE PARTY **BEGIN**!
OH... UM... SORRY. DID YOU WANT SOME?

MR. BUTTS, DID THE CONGRESSIONAL WITCH HUNTS MAKE LIFE DIFFICULT FOR YOU AND YOUR FAMILY?
DID THEY?...

"IT WAS A **NIGHTMARE**! FROM THE LATE NIGHT VISITS FROM NICO-NAZIS...

"...TO THE **RELENTLESS** PERSECUTION FROM THE PRESS!"
WHAT DO YOU **WANT** FROM ME?

ARE YOU OKAY NOW?
NOT REALLY. I NEED TIME TO HEAL.
©B Trudeau

SO THE RISK OF GETTING CANCER?
STILL UNPROVEN!

THEN HOW ABOUT THE STUDIES YOU SUPPRESSED?
WHAT?
Generic famous PIZZA

UM... MR. CHAIRMAN, THAT QUESTION DOESN'T SEEM TO ME TO BE IN THE SPIRIT OF THE NEW CONGRESSIONAL UNDERSIGHT!

UM... SORRY. IT WAS FROM THE OLD PLAYBOOK...
ZOUNDS, SIR! GET A GRIP ON THE REINS OF POWER!
©B Trudeau

YOU KNOW, KIDS, THERE JUST DOESN'T SEEM TO BE ANY **END** TO THE EXCITEMENT SURROUNDING THE PRESIDENTIAL ASPIRATIONS OF SENATOR **PHIL GRAMM**!

WHO IS THIS HOPEFUL FROM THE HEART OF TEXAS? TO HIS COLLEAGUES, HE'S JUST PLAIN PHIL— THE SOFT-SPOKEN COUNTRY BOY WITH THE CROOKED GRIN AND DANCING EYES!

AND YET THERE IS A DARKER SIDE! ASK HIM ABOUT HIS CLANDESTINE SUPPORT OF THE ARYAN NATION, AND YOU'RE MET WITH A STONY SILENCE! BRING UP THE RUMORS OF CAMPAIGN PAYOFFS, AND HE'S OUT THE DOOR!

AND THEN THERE ARE HIS POSITIONS: **FOR** PRIVATE OWNERSHIP OF AUTOMATIC WEAPONS; **FOR** ABOLISHING SOCIAL SECURITY; **FOR** REPEALING THE FIRST AMENDMENT; **FOR** THE DEATH PENALTY FOR ABORTIONISTS!
AND THERE'S **MORE**! BACK AFTER THIS!

UM... MARK?
YO.

I'M ALMOST POSITIVE NONE OF THAT'S TRUE.
WHO CARES? RUSH HAS FREED UP THIS BUSINESS!
GB Trudeau

MIKE, SOMETIME YOU'RE GOING TO HAVE TO EXPLAIN TO ME ABOUT THIS "ANGRY, WHITE MALE" WHO PUT NEWT AND COMPANY OVER THE TOP...

I MEAN, WHO IS THIS JERK, ANYWAY?

UM... WELL, ACTUALLY...
©B Trudeau

OH, GOD, NO...
LET ME EXPLAIN...

I DIDN'T HEAR YOU CORRECTLY, MIKE. YOU COULDN'T POSSIBLY HAVE JUST TOLD ME THAT YOU VOTED REPUBLICAN!

J.J., I CAN EXPLAIN...
EXPLAIN? HOW CAN YOU EXPLAIN JOINING THE PARTY OF PRO-LIFERS, GUN NUTS AND RELIGIOUS BIGOTS!

IT'S NOT THAT SIMPLE, J.J. ...
SURE IT IS! LIFE-LONG LIBERAL ABANDONS PRINCIPLES, BECOMES A REPUBLICAN!

A ROCKEFELLER REPUBLICAN! YOU'LL HARDLY NOTICE ANY DIFFERENCE!
MICHAEL, YOU STOOGE! THAT'S HOW IT STARTS!
©B Trudeau

I CAN'T BELIEVE MY EARS HERE, MICHAEL...
LOOK, J.J. DRIFTING A LITTLE TO THE RIGHT HAS A LOT OF ADVANTAGES...

FOR INSTANCE, CONSERVATISM MAKES IT POSSIBLE TO TRANSFORM YOUR DEEPEST FEARS INTO OPEN CONVICTIONS!

LIKE WHAT, MIKE? WHAT ARE WE REALLY TALKING ABOUT HERE?
WELL, LIKE THE RELATIONSHIP BETWEEN RACE AND CRIME.
©B Trudeau

WHAT?
OF COURSE, YOU STILL HAVE TO TALK IN CODE.

J.J., I DON'T KNOW WHAT YOU'RE GETTING SO WORKED UP OVER. IT'S NOT LIKE I JOINED THE RADICAL RIGHT...

BESIDES, I STILL HOLD THE SAME CORE CONVICTIONS AND PRINCIPLES I ALWAYS HAVE!

I MEAN, I STILL OPPOSE DISCRIMINATION, I STILL SUPPORT REPRODUCTIVE FREEDOM, I'M STILL GIVING TO ANTI-GUN GROUPS...

HOW ABOUT LESBIAN ARTISTS' RIGHTS?
UM... OKAY, I DID STOP PAYMENT ON THAT ONE CHECK.

J.J., I DON'T SEE WHAT THE BIG DEAL IS HERE — IT'S ONLY POLITICS...

WELL, EXCUSE ME, MIKE, BUT WHEN YOU'VE LIVED WITH SOMEONE FOR A LONG TIME, IT'S A **BIT** OF A SHOCK TO WAKE UP AND SUDDENLY FIND THAT...

...THAT...
WHAT?

HOW LONG HAVE YOU BEEN WEARING SUSPENDERS?
FIVE YEARS.

YOU KNOW, THE IRONY OF THIS IS THAT EVEN THOUGH I VOTED REPUBLICAN, I DON'T REALLY **FEEL** ALL THAT CONSERVATIVE...

I STILL FEEL GOVERNMENT CAN IMPROVE PEOPLE'S LIVES. BUT WHAT WE'VE BEEN DOING JUST HASN'T BEEN WORKING!

WHAT I'VE BEEN FEELING LATELY IS A DEEP YEARNING FOR A RETURN TO ACCOUNTABILITY, TO SANITY, TO CIVILITY — JUST LIKE **MOST** PEOPLE!

WELL... I GUESS YOU'VE **ALWAYS** BEEN LIKE MOST PEOPLE.
HEY, **SOMEONE'S** GOTTA BE IN THE MAINSTREAM!

MIKE!
HEY, REV! I WAS UP IN THE AREA SEEING A CLIENT AND THOUGHT I'D STOP BY!

WHAT A GREAT SURPRISE! JUST LOOK AT YOU— YOU HAVEN'T CHANGED A BIT!
YES, I HAVE. I VOTED G.O.P. THIS YEAR!

YOU WHAT? OH, MIKE...

QUICK, COME IN BEFORE YOU'RE SEEN.
YOU'D HARBOR A REPUBLICAN?

DO YOU WANT TO TALK ABOUT IT, MIKE? OR IS IT STILL TOO PAINFUL?
NOT AT ALL. IN FACT, I'M PRETTY COMFORTABLE ABOUT THE WHOLE THING.

I GUESS I'D JUST LOST FAITH IN THE DEMOCRATS' ABILITY TO IMPROVE OUR LIVES. EVERYTHING SEEMED WORSE THAN EVER. IT WAS A SURPRISINGLY EASY CALL.

UH-HUH...

OKAY, WHAT REALLY HAPPENED, SON? WERE YOU MUGGED?
UM... YEAH, TWICE. DO YOU THINK THERE'S A CONNECTION?

MIKE, IT SOUNDS LIKE YOU'RE SUFFERING FROM URBAN STRESS SYNDROME. BUT TURNING REPUBLICAN ISN'T THE ANSWER...

DURING THE '80S, UNDER TWO G.O.P. PRESIDENTS, THE U.S. PRISON POPULATION DOUBLED! DO YOU FEEL SAFER?

REPUBLICANS ONLY WANT TO PUNISH PEOPLE FOR BAD CHOICES. THE DEMOCRATIC APPROACH IS TO PROMOTE HOPE AND PREVENT BAD CHOICES IN THE FIRST PLACE!

SPEAKER NEWT SAYS THAT'S A HIPPIE LIE, SPEAKER NEWT SAYS...
UH-OH...

REV, I GUESS I WAS JUST TIRED OF FEELING GUILTY OVER SOCIETY'S WOES, OVER OTHER PEOPLE'S MISTAKES...

MIKE, GUILT IS PART OF WHAT HOLDS SOCIETY TOGETHER. WITH-OUT IT, WE'D HAVE MORAL CHAOS.

WELL, THAT WOULD ACCOUNT FOR THE SHAME...
WHAT SHAME?

THE SHAME I FEEL OVER NOT FEELING GUILTY.
MIKE, ARE YOU SURE YOU'RE READY TO BE A REPUBLICAN?
©B Trudeau

YOU SEE, REV, I BELIEVE THAT THE WHOLE ISSUE OF PERSONAL RESPONSIBILITY GOT AWAY FROM US...

AN EXPLOSION OF "RIGHTS" DISRUPTED THE COVENANT BETWEEN CITIZENRY AND GOVERNMENT. MY VOTE EX-PRESSED A LONGING TO RESTORE THAT BALANCE.

SO HAVE YOU BOUGHT YOUR WHITE BELT AND MADRAS SLACKS YET?
ON ORDER. YOU'RE NOT TAKING THIS WELL, ARE YOU?
©B Trudeau

THE WAY I SEE IT, REV, THE DEMO-CRATIC PARTY STOPPED GETTING TRACTION YEARS AGO...

THE DEMOCRATS NEEDED A BLOW-OUT TO FORCE THEM TO RE-FOCUS, TO RE-CONNECT WITH PEOPLE'S LIVES...

THAT'S BASICALLY WHAT MY VOTE WAS ABOUT—TO HELP THE CAUSE I GREW UP WITH!

SO IT WAS A TOUGH-LOVE VOTE?
EXACTLY. THE PARTY JUST NEEDS SOME TIME TO ITSELF.
©B Trudeau

LACEY!
WHY, NEWT, DEAR—WAS MY DOOR OPEN?

WHO CARES? I NEED YOU!
DEAR MAN, WEREN'T YOU EVER TAUGHT NOT TO BARGE INTO A LADY'S CHAMBERS UNANNOUNCED?

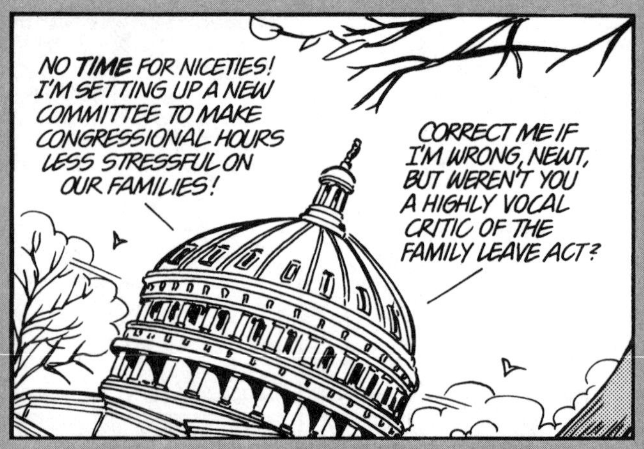
NO TIME FOR NICETIES! I'M SETTING UP A NEW COMMITTEE TO MAKE CONGRESSIONAL HOURS LESS STRESSFUL ON OUR FAMILIES!
CORRECT ME IF I'M WRONG, NEWT, BUT WEREN'T YOU A HIGHLY VOCAL CRITIC OF THE FAMILY LEAVE ACT?

I DON'T TAKE YOUR POINT.
AND DO YOU REALLY THINK SOMEONE WITH A LURID HISTORY OF DIVORCE, CHILD SUPPORT AND ALIMONY PROBLEMS SHOULD BE LEADING THIS EFFORT?

HEY! LOTS OF NORMAL AMERICANS HAVE PROBLEMATIC PERSONAL LIVES!
MAYBE, NEWT, BUT THEY'RE NOT ALL POSING AS THE RIGHTEOUS NEW FACE OF AMERICAN FAMILY VALUES! GOOD DAY, SIR!

WHY, YOU HIPPIE! TRAITOR! McGOV...
WHOOM!
DON'T YOU SNAP AT ME, YOUNG MAN! WHO RAISED YOU, WOLVES?
©B Trudeau

AS ALL EYES TURN TOWARD THE TRIAL OF THE CENTURY...
WE'LL BE BACK WITH **ALL-NEW O.J.** AFTER THIS!

O.J. T-SHIRTS
YO, **MOVE** IT! LET'S GET THESE SHIRTS **UNPACKED!**
STYLE O.J.
T-SHIRTS

JEFF! GOT YOUR DEAL MEMO ON MY O.J. CLIENTS! LET'S GO TO CONTRACT!

...THE PLAYERS PREPARE!
THINK MY TAN IS EVEN ENOUGH YET?
FOR AN ALTERNATE? SURE.

WHAT'S UP, BLOND PERSON?
NOTHING. JUST PICKING OUT MY WARDROBE.

FOR THE TRIAL OF THE CENTURY?
UH-HUH. I WANT TO LOOK MY BEST FOR OPENING ARGUMENTS!

I'VE GOT TO BE CAREFUL. SOME OF MY STUFF DOESN'T WORK ON HUNK-RA...

YOU'RE DRESSING FOR TWO?
HAVE TO. THAT'S WHY I'M THINKING LYCRA.

LET ME TELL YOU WHY GETTING MY OUTFIT RIGHT IS SO CRITICAL, ZONK...

I'M GOING TO BE SEEN ON TELEVISION ALL OVER THE **WORLD!** IT'S VERY IMPORTANT THAT I MAKE A STRONG FIRST IMPRESSION DURING OPENING ARGUMENTS...

IT ISN'T JUST A FASHION CHOICE—IT'S A **CAREER** MOVE! I HAVE TO ASK MYSELF, WHAT WOULD MERYL STREEP WEAR?

ISN'T THAT PUTTING A LOT OF PRESSURE ON YOURSELF?
MAYBE. BUT I'M **TIRED** OF LIVING IN HER SHADOW!

HMM... THIS IS SUCH A TOUGH FASHION CALL!
BETTER TO GET IT RIGHT. AS AN O.J. ALTERNATE, YOU'RE GOING TO BE PART OF HISTORY!

YEAH, I GUESS...
YOU GUESS? YOU DON'T SOUND VERY EXCITED.

WELL, YOU HAVE TO UNDER-STAND, ZONK. IN A PREVIOUS LIFE, I WAS CATHERINE THE GREAT. MY PLACE IN HISTORY HAS ALREADY BEEN ASSURED.

OH, GOSH, THAT SOUNDED REALLY CONCEITED, DIDN'T IT?
A LITTLE, YEAH.
©B Trudeau

OKAY, THIS IS THE FINAL CUT! WHAT DO YOU THINK?
UM...

I'M PAIRING A MAUVE LYCRA TANK TOP WITH A GOLD BRO-CADE VEST, APRICOT LEG-GINGS AND WHITE HEELS...

...AND, OF COURSE, LACY UNDERGAR-MENTS! I HOPE JUDGE ITO AP-PROVES!
OF THE LACY UNDER-GAR-MENTS?
©B Trudeau

NO, NO, OF THE WHOLE LOOK! I THINK IT SAYS, "1995!" I THINK IT SAYS, "NOW!"
I THINK IT SAYS, "HI, SAILOR!"

WELL, THAT'S IT— ALL PACKED AND READY FOR DAY ONE OF THE TRIAL!

GOT MY OUTFIT, MY BEAUTY PRODUCTS, MY BLOW-DRYER, LOTS OF SNACKS ... OH, I NEED SOMETHING TO READ!

OH, THAT RE-MINDS ME. I PICKED YOU UP AN "ENQUIR-ER" TO TAKE.
ZONKER, YOU KNOW I'M NOT ALLOWED NEWSPAPERS.
©B Trudeau

IT'S OKAY— I CUT OUT THE O.J. STORIES!
THAT'S SO SWEET...

LETTERS, LETTERS, LETTERS! YOU WRITE 'EM, WE IGNORE 'EM!
EXCEPT DURING **THIS WEEK**!

THAT'S RIGHT, IT'S TIME FOR OUR ANNUAL **READERS' MAILBAG**! ZONKER, WHY DON'T YOU START US OFF?

HAPPY TO, MIKE! FROM G.K. IN MINNEAPOLIS COMES THIS—"DEAR BOYS: THANKS FOR A GREAT WEEK OF LETTERS. YOU HANDLED THE TOUGH QUESTIONS BRILLIANTLY!"

ZONKER, THAT'S SATURDAY'S LETTER...
I KNOW, I SWITCHED THE ORDER. WE NEEDED A STRONGER OPENING.

WE'RE BACK WITH OUR ANNUAL **READERS' MAIL-BAG**! CARE TO HANDLE OUR NEXT LETTER, MARCUS?
YOU GOT IT, MIKE!

L.Z. FROM TUPELO WRITES: "DEAR GUYS: WHAT HAPPENED TO ZONKER? HE WAS IN YESTER-DAY'S STRIP, AND NOW HE'S GONE. WHAT'S THE DEAL?"

WELL, L.Z., THE TRUTH IS HE WAS REPLACED. THE DEMANDS OF THE MATERIAL SHIFTED, BECOMING LESS WHIMSICAL, SO A HARDER-EDGED CHARACTER WAS BROUGHT IN TO TAKE OVER.

IT MAY SEEM A LITTLE UNFAIR...
BUT HEY—IT HAPPENS!

HERE'S A **TECHNICAL** INQUIRY, MARK! "DEAR DOONESPEOPLE: HOW DO YOU GET THAT WAY COOL SHADING EFFECT? THINE, DAVID IN DES MOINES."

WELL, DAVID, THE SHORT ANSWER IS PATIENCE! EACH DOT IN AN AREA LIKE MARK'S SHIRT IS HAND DRAWN AND INKED IN ONE OF OUR OFFSHORE STUDIOS...

IT'S PAINSTAKING WORK, BUT THE GRAPHIC EFFECT IS SO STRIKING, WE THINK IT'S WORTH THE EXTRA TROUBLE AND COST!

UNLESS, OF COURSE, THEY SHADE THE WRONG AREA.
WHICH **NEVER** HAPPENS!

"DEAR GUYS: A FEW WEEKS AGO, YOU INVITED READERS TO E-MAIL YOU TO FIND OUT HOW TO JOIN THE 'COGNITIVE ELITE' OF OUR NEW INFORMATION SOCIETY..."

"WHAT KIND OF RESPONSE DID YOU GET? CURIOUS IN KANSAS."
WELL, CURIOUS, NEARLY 10,000 OF YOU MESSAGED US, AND THEY ALL RECEIVED THE FOLLOWING REPLY...

"DEAR READER: REGRET TO ADVISE THAT YOU ARE UNLIKELY TO JOIN THE NEW COGNITIVE ELITE: YOU HAVE TOO MUCH TIME ON YOUR HANDS. SINCERELY, MIKE."

SOME OF YOU WERE NOT AMUSED.
AND WROTE **AGAIN** TO SAY SO!
©B Trudeau

"DEAR MIKE: HOW COME YOU GUYS **NEVER** DO ANY JOKES ABOUT THE POST OFFICE?..."
U.S.M

"POST OFFICE JOKES REALLY CRACK ME UP. AND WHAT WITH THE NEW RATE INCREASE, A POST OFFICE JOKE WOULD BE REALLY TIMELY NOW..."

"SO COULD YOU DO ONE? YOURS, PHIL."
DEPENDS. WHAT'S THE POSTMARK ON THAT LETTER?

UM... JUNE 14, 1973.
NO CHARGE, PHIL!
©B Trudeau

LISTEN TO THIS ONE, MIKE! "DEAR GUYS: I'VE NOTICED YOU RARELY DEPICT VIOLENCE. WHAT'S THE DEAL? SIGNED, MICK FROM CHICAGO."

WHY DON'T WE HAVE MORE VIOLENCE? WELL, FOR ONE THING, IT'S HARDER TO DRAW...
BUT MORE IMPORTANT, IT'S AGAINST EVERYTHING THIS FAMILY FEATURE STANDS FOR!

CRANG!

DON'T WORRY—IT WAS JUST A HARMLESS **TOON** SAFE!
YOU SEE, WE HAVE A RESPONSIBILITY TO KIDS!
©B Trudeau

BUT, SIR, WON'T YOUR WELFARE REFORM PROGRAM ONLY FURTHER DESTABILIZE THE VERY FAMILIES THAT MOST NEED TO BE STRENGTHENED?

NO! THAT'S A TYPICAL MISREPRESENTATION FROM THE LIBERAL MEDIA! YOU PEOPLE ARE STILL TRYING TO DESTROY ME!

BUT, SIR...
ELITIST! HIPPIE! TRAITOR!
BZZZ!
HOLD IT, I GOT A CALL...

WHAT IS IT, MARY?
SIR, THERE'S A GENTLEMAN HERE TO SEE YOU ABOUT SETTING UP A PILOT ORPHANAGE PROGRAM.

PILOT ORPHANAGE PROGRAM?
YES, SIR. HE SAYS HE HAS AN APPOINTMENT.

MAY I HAVE YOUR NAME AGAIN, SIR?
DUKE. FATHER DUKE.

REFRESH MY MEMORY, REVEREND—WHAT'S THIS ABOUT?
YOUR ORPHANAGE PLAN, MR. SPEAKER...

THE MAIN DRAWBACK IS COST—ABOUT 40 GRAND A KID, RIGHT? WELL, I CAN GET THE JOB DONE FOR LESS THAN 20!

20? ARE YOU SURE?
YES, SIR. AND IF YOU'LL FUND MY PILOT PROGRAM, I'LL **PROVE** IT!

HMM... WHAT'D YOU SAY YOUR NAME WAS AGAIN?
DUKE. FATHER DUKE.

SO YOU THINK YOU CAN RUN A COST-EFFECTIVE ORPHANAGE, FATHER?
I **KNOW** IT, SIR!

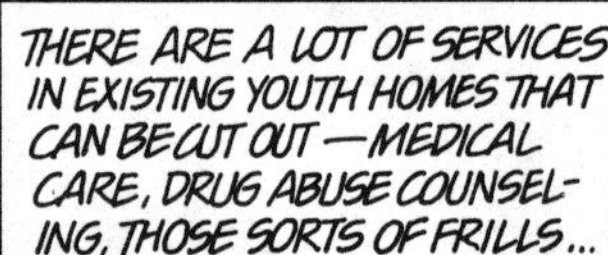
THERE ARE A LOT OF SERVICES IN EXISTING YOUTH HOMES THAT CAN BE CUT OUT—MEDICAL CARE, DRUG ABUSE COUNSELING, THOSE SORTS OF FRILLS...

BUT MOST IMPORTANT, I'D CUT LABOR COSTS BY GETTING THE KIDS INVOLVED IN THEIR OWN KEEP—YOU KNOW, FOOD PREPARATION, MAINTENANCE, YARD WORK, ETC.

OF COURSE, WE'D HAVE TO ADJUST THE CHILD LABOR LAWS...
LIBERAL CHILD LABOR LAWS! SURELY THAT'S NOT A PROBLEM?

YOU SEE, MR. SPEAKER, I HAVE A VISION—I SEE A NATIONAL CHAIN OF WELL-MANAGED, FOR-PROFIT ORPHANAGES FOR SOCIETY'S SMALLEST CAST-OFFS!

IN SUCH A FACILITY, WE REAR AND DISCIPLINE EACH CHILD IN A WHOLESOME, VALUES-RICH ENVIRONMENT FROM WHICH THERE IS NO ESCAPE! THAT'S MY VISION.

SOUNDS GREAT, FATHER, REALLY GREAT!
THANKS.

I'M ONLY SORRY MY OWN KIDS ARE TOO OLD.
MY SOLE REGRET AS WELL.

SO WHAT QUALIFICATIONS DO YOU BRING TO YOUR WORK, FATHER?
I'M A SHEPHERD BY CALLING, MR. SPEAKER...

I'VE ALWAYS GONE WHERE I THOUGHT I COULD DO THE LORD'S WORK — SAMOA, CHINA, HAITI, KUWAIT — I'VE FELT OTHER PEOPLE'S PAIN ALL OVER THE WORLD!

BUT MOST IMPORTANT, I'VE FELT MY OWN PAIN. AS A FORMER ORPHAN MYSELF, MY LIFE HAS BEEN FILLED WITH HARDSHIP, HOPE AND REDEMPTION — ALMOST LIKE A MOVIE!

"BOYS TOWN"?
NO, MORE LIKE "DIE HARD I" MEETS "DIE HARD II."

...AND I'D LIKE TO START WITH 50 KIDS RIGHT AWAY — WITH YOUR BLESSING, OF COURSE.

AND WHAT DO YOU INTEND TO CALL YOUR FACILITY?
I'M CALLING IT "FATHER DUKE'S HOME FOR MARGINALIZED MUNCHKINS."

KIND OF A MOUTHFUL, ISN'T IT?
YOU'RE RIGHT. HOW ABOUT "DUKE'S PLACE"?

SOUNDS LIKE A BAR.
I'VE GOT IT — HOW ABOUT "NOTHIN' BUT ORPHANS"?

I WANT TO THANK YOU FOR YOUR SUPPORT OF "NOTHIN' BUT ORPHANS," MR. SPEAKER!

NOT AT ALL. WHEN DO YOU PROPOSE STARTING?
JUST AS SOON AS THE CHECK CLEARS...

I'VE GOT A WONDERFUL SITE PICKED OUT FOR OUR PILOT FACILITY — MOUNTAIN SETTING, CLEAN, FRESH AIR — THE KIDS'LL LOVE IT!

HELLO, MR. DUKE'S RESIDENCE.
HONEY, CLEAN OUT THE ATTIC!

SIR! YOU'RE HOME!
GET UP, HONEY. I WANT TO DO SOMETHING I'VE BEEN MEANING TO FOR YEARS.

WHAT'S THAT, SIR?
RELAX, I'M NOT GOING TO HIT YOU. CLOSE YOUR EYES.

©B Trudeau
SIR! YOU'RE HOME!
GET UP, HONEY. I NEED YOU TO PAINT THE HOUSE.

UP AND AT 'EM, HONEY! WE'VE GOT AN ORPHANAGE TO GET READY!

GASP!
WHAT? WHAT'S WRONG?

SIR, YOU'VE... YOU'VE JOINED THE **PRIESTHOOD!**
GOOD EYE.
©B Trudeau

I DROVE YOU TO IT, DIDN'T I, SIR?
WHAT DO **YOU** CARE? I THOUGHT YOU PEOPLE WERE GODLESS.

...ANYWAY, BY LETTING THE OLDER KIDS WORK OFF THEIR KEEP, I FIGURE I CAN CLEAR $17,000 AN ORPHAN— **AFTER** TAXES!

AND WHERE EXACTLY DO I FIT INTO THIS PLAN, SIR?
WELL, INITIALLY, I FIGURED YOU'D BE DEN MOTHER...
Nothin' but Orphans Inc.

...BUT THEN I THOUGHT, HEY, SHE'S ASIAN—KNOWS HER NUMBERS! MIGHT AS WELL LET HER COOK THE BOOKS!

I BEG YOUR PARDON?
I'D DO IT, BUT MY MATH STINKS. I ALWAYS GET CAUGHT.
©B Trudeau

I CLEANED THE ATTIC, SIR, BUT I JUST DON'T SEE HOW YOU COULD FIT MORE THAN THREE BEDS UP THERE...

YOU ADD THAT TO FOUR IN THE GUEST ROOM, AND YOU'RE LOOKING AT A TOP CAPACITY OF SEVEN KIDS!

WAIT A MINUTE- WHAT ABOUT **MY** BEDROOM? THAT'S BIG ENOUGH FOR ANOTHER SIX COTS-**EASY!**

BUT WHERE WILL **YOU** STAY?
IN THE BAHAMAS. DON'T WORRY, I'LL BE FINE.
©B Trudeau

...AND I THOUGHT IF YOU COULD MOVE THESE AMMO PALLETS OUT, SIR, WE COULD STORE INFANT FORMULA RIGHT HERE.

DOES THAT WORK FOR YOU, SIR?... SIR? WHERE ARE YOU?
OVER HERE...

I'M CHECKING OUT THE CRAWL SPACE BEHIND THE FURNACE!
©B Trudeau

UM... WHAT FOR?
I THINK WE CAN FIT ANOTHER TWO CRIBS BACK HERE.
Nothin' but Orphans Inc.

I MEASURED IT OUT, HONEY, AND I THINK WE CAN FIT TWO CRIBS IN THE CRAWL SPACE BEHIND THE FURNACE...
YOU CAN'T DO THAT, SIR.

OH NO? WHY NOT?
BECAUSE THE BABIES MIGHT ASPHYXIATE, OR THEIR CRIBS MIGHT CATCH FIRE AND THEY COULD BURN TO DEATH.

©B Trudeau

YOU'RE NOT GOING TO BE A BIG PAIN IN THE BUTT ABOUT MY ORPHANAGE, ARE YOU, HONEY?
>GASP!< YOU CAN **SAY** THAT WORD? AS A PRIEST?

THIS IS ROLAND HEDLEY. IN THE MONTHS AHEAD, THIS FINE FEATURE WILL BE SWITCHING TO AN **ALL-O.J. FORMAT!** I'LL BE BREAKING THE BIG STORIES...
...WHILE I HANDLE ANALYSIS OF THE LARGER **SOCIAL** ISSUES RAISED!

TO SUPPLEMENT THE PRESS COVERAGE, I'LL BE OFFERING A **FIRST-HAND** ACCOUNT FROM THE JURY BOX...
...AS WILL **I**!

...BOTH OF WHOM ARE REPPED BY YOURS TRULY, AGENT TO A HOT LINE-UP OF **MAJOR** O.J. PLAYERS!
...INCLUDING ME, A FORMER PRO ATHLETE WITH PLENTY OF IN-SIGHT INTO THE VIOLENT UNDERSIDE OF SPORTS!

...AND ME, BOTH PEACE OFFICER AND AFRICAN AMERICAN! I'LL BE PROVIDING PUNGENT COMMENTARY ON THE RACIAL DIMENSIONS OF O.J.'S TRIAL RIGHT UP TO HIS ACQUITTAL!

...WHILE I HANDLE **COLOR** DUTIES! AS A NATIVE CALI-FORNIAN, I'LL MAKE SENSE OF THE LOCAL ZEITGEIST— **AND** TRANSLATE THE TRIAL TESTIMONY OF FELLOW DUDE "KATO" KAELIN!

SO FOR WALL-TO-WALL O.J. COVERAGE...
...THINK **TEAM DOONESBURY!**
WE'RE THE **O.J. SPECIALISTS!**
GB Trudeau

SEQUESTRATION.
SO WHAT'S IT LIKE?
LONELY, B.D....

I'M STUCK IN THIS DEPRESSING LITTLE ROOM WITH NO CABLE.
WHERE'S THE HOTEL?

I DON'T KNOW. THEY BRING US HERE BY THIS LONG, ROUNDABOUT ROUTE.
WHAT DO YOU SEE FROM THE WINDOW?

NOT MUCH. A PICKUP JUST FLOATED BY.
OKAY, SO YOU'RE STILL IN CALIFORNIA...
©B. Trudeau

SEQUESTRATION, CONT'D.
DOESN'T ANYTHING LOOK FAMILIAR?
WELL, THERE'S A McDONALD'S AND AN ARBY'S AND A HERTZ...

HELL, YOU COULD BE IN MEXICO!
DON'T WORRY–YOU'LL FIND OUT WHERE WE ARE SOON ENOUGH!

HOW DO YOU FIGURE?
THE PRESS, B.D.! THE CREAM OF U.S. JOURNALISM WILL BE WORKING DAY AND NIGHT TO TRACK US DOWN!
©B. Trudeau

GOOD MORNING, BEVERLY HILLS HOTEL.
YEAH, YOU GOT A PARTY OF 24 REGISTERED? MYSTERIOUS, MIXED-RACE?

SO WHO ARE YOU ROOMING WITH, BOOPSIE?
NOBODY, B.D.—WE'RE NOT EVEN ALLOWED TO TALK TO ONE ANOTHER...

...EXCEPT DURING MEALS, WHEN WE'RE SUPERVISED. THE REST OF THE TIME WE'RE ALONE IN OUR ROOMS.

THEY DO AIR US ONCE IN A WHILE. LAST WEEKEND, THE DEPUTIES MADE US ALL GO TO A KENNY G CONCERT.
©B. Trudeau

BRUTAL. WAS THERE AN INCIDENT?
NO, WE ALL WENT PEACEFULLY. NO ONE WANTS TO GET IN TROUBLE.

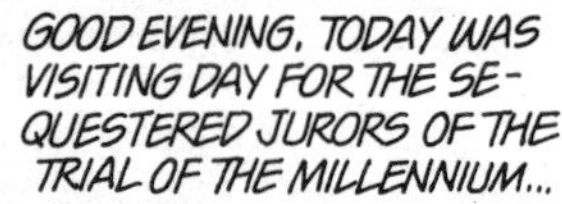
GOOD EVENING. TODAY WAS VISITING DAY FOR THE SE-QUESTERED JURORS OF THE TRIAL OF THE MILLENNIUM...

LOVED ONES ASSEMBLED AT A PRE-ARRANGED LOCATION AND WERE THEN SHUTTLED TO THE JURY'S TOP-SECRET HIDEOUT!

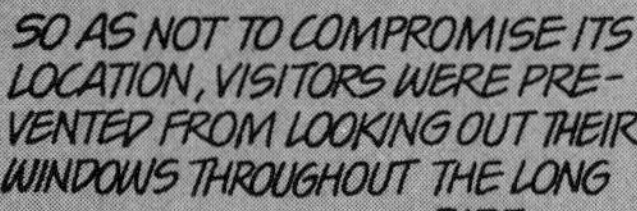
SO AS NOT TO COMPROMISE ITS LOCATION, VISITORS WERE PRE-VENTED FROM LOOKING OUT THEIR WINDOWS THROUGHOUT THE LONG RIDE.

WHERE DO YOU WANT HIM, MA'AM?
I AM NOT HAPPY.
LEMME SEE...

YOU CAN TAKE THE SACK OFF NOW, B.D. — YOU'RE HERE!
HOW HUMILI-ATING...

WORTH IT, I HOPE.
I GUESS. SO HOW'S THE TRIAL OF THE CENTURY GOING?

B.D.! ARE YOU TRYING TO GET ME THROWN OFF THE JURY? I CAN'T BREATHE A WORD ABOUT THE TRIAL!

I CAN'T EVEN MENTION THE 15TH AND THE 10TH LETTERS OF THE ALPHABET!
OKAY, OKAY, I'M SORRY.

MAN, I SEE WHAT YOU MEAN ABOUT THE ACCOMMODATIONS. WHAT A DUMP!
YEAH, IT'S A LITTLE DEPRESS-ING...

SO HOW DO YOU PASS THE TIME?
WELL, I READ A LOT OF HARLE-QUINS. THE DRUG STORE DELIVERS THEM...

EXCUSE ME, FOLKS — TIME'S UP.
WHAT? I JUST GOT HERE! WHAT ABOUT CON-VIVIAL TIME?

CONJUGAL TIME? SORRY.
JUST GIVE US THREE MINUTES! FIVE, TOPS!
PUT YOUR SACK BACK ON, B.D.

O.J. CITY... CENTER OF THE UNIVERSE...

NATIONAL DESK!
HEY, BOSS, IT'S RICK.

OUR MAN IN O.J. CITY! TELL ME SOMETHING I DIDN'T READ ON THE WIRES YESTERDAY!
IF YOU INSIST...

ONE OF MY SOURCES AT THE JAILHOUSE BROUGHT ME SOME-THING MIND-BOGGLING LAST NIGHT...

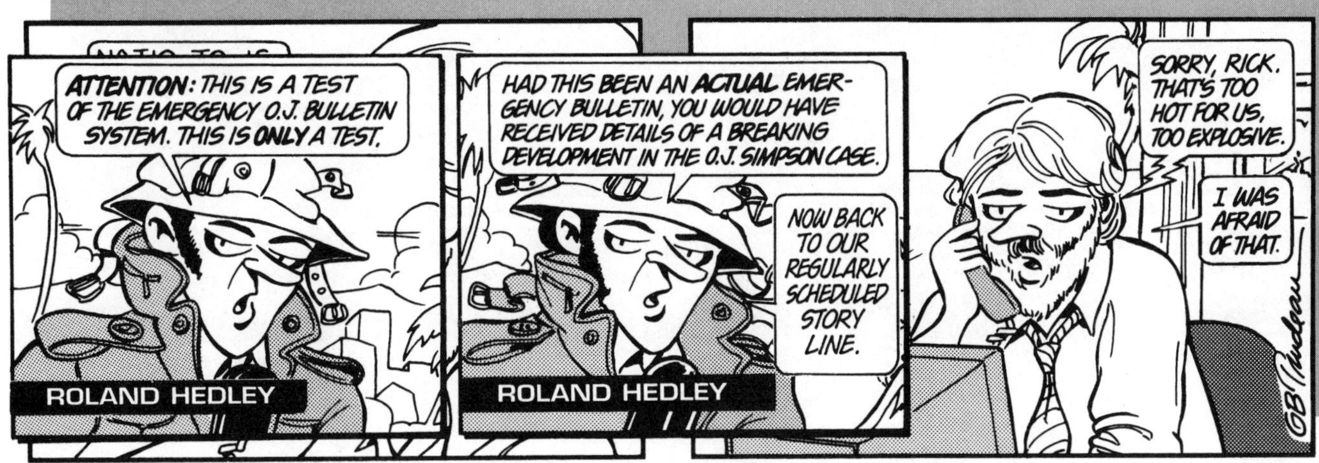
ATTENTION: THIS IS A TEST OF THE EMERGENCY O.J. BULLETIN SYSTEM. THIS IS ONLY A TEST.
ROLAND HEDLEY
HAD THIS BEEN AN ACTUAL EMER-GENCY BULLETIN, YOU WOULD HAVE RECEIVED DETAILS OF A BREAKING DEVELOPMENT IN THE O.J. SIMPSON CASE.
NOW BACK TO OUR REGULARLY SCHEDULED STORY LINE.
ROLAND HEDLEY
SORRY, RICK. THAT'S TOO HOT FOR US, TOO EXPLOSIVE.
I WAS AFRAID OF THAT.